INTENSIVE FAITH

DAN FINFROCK

*True stories of one man's attempt
to walk by faith*

PUBLISHED BY

Intensive Care Ministries

P.O. Box 109, Mentone, California 92359
Phone 909-798-0451

www.icmbible.com

❖ ❖ ❖ ❖ ❖

Having experienced many missionary ventures over the last 30 years in many of the same countries I found Intensive Faith to be a heart pounding, hard to put down account of how God used Dan and Debbie in Intensive Care Ministries. It is a captivating true story of the many challenges, setbacks, tragedies and unexpected adventures that have shaped their daily lives, since they made themselves available to the Author of our Faith. It is an inspiring and riveting reminder, to every believer, of what God can do with any man or woman who is willing to say, "Yes Lord, send me!"

Lloyd Pulley

Calvary Chapel Old Bridge

❖ ❖ ❖ ❖ ❖

What a powerful testimony of God's work in your life, Dan. Reading through this adventure story, I stood in awe at God's sovereign intervention into the affairs of His servants. Intensive Faith is certainly a faith-builder. To God be all glory.

Neal Pirolo

Emmaus Road International

❖ ❖ ❖ ❖ ❖

A Word
as You Begin

This is a simple book, because I am simple man.
This is a telling book, because I have adventures to tell.
We all have a story that longs to be told; I am no exception.

I've had the privilege of listening to great Bible teachers, inspiring speakers, and have read countless biographies of faithful men and women through the ages who had gone before us. Simple threads of truth run through each of their lives. Threads of truth, such as: Love God with all your heart, soul, mind, and strength; read his Word; pray without ceasing and take steps of faith as He presents them.

I hope as you read these adventures of faith you will find a thread or two that will strengthen and encourage you. And may the stories you have to tell be filled with simple truths made flesh as you follow His plan, in His way, in His time.

Sincerely,

Pastor Dan Finfrock

CONTENTS

❖ ❖ ❖ ❖ ❖

PROLOGUE
Bangladesh 1995

The chilling sound of hostile male voices shook me awake at 2:30 A.M. Scrambling to the window, I saw dark figures and vague shadows darting about outside. Although I didn't know what stirred up such an angry beehive, I feared it had something to do with me. My heart banged in my rib cage.

Crossing to another window, I asked others in the house about the commotion, but no one would answer. One look at their faces, however, told me all I needed to know: We were in trouble.

Men speaking in the Bengali language yelled, "Where is the American? Give us the American!" Word quickly spread that bandits had crept into our countryside village in Bangladesh, captured the guards, and tied them up. They planned to kidnap me and demand $13,000 in ransom.

Until I flew into the crowded city of Dhaka for the first time in 1995, I thought I had seen real poverty during my six years living in the Philippines. Yet nothing could have prepared me for the utter destitution of Bangladesh, one of the poorest countries in the world.

More than 170 million people cram the streets and countryside of this impoverished nation, all living in a space less than half the size of California. Scores of people sleep in the streets. The stench of defecation permeates the air. Filth and pollution soil Dhaka, the capitol city. Trucks, buses, and cars belch black clouds of smoke. It seems to take forever to get anywhere as you weave through congested streets, wobbly rickshaws, and thin cattle.

My host for this visit, John Biswas of Bengali Ministries, had gathered a group of his pastors and leaders for the Inductive Bible Study seminar I came to teach. I developed the course, which teaches an effective system of study, during my years in the Philippines. Now I began to venture out, presenting it in other Third World countries.

On our arrival in Dhaka we rented a car; its air-conditioning worked for thirty minutes, then died. For the rest of our twelve-hour journey we rode in stifling humidity. Five hours into the trek we needed to take a one-hour ferry across a bay. Trucks and buses rushed to cram onto the boat. Four drivers argued vehemently for the last two spots, looking like they were ready for a fistfight. Our timid driver stood back so we ended up waiting two hours for another ferry. Finally, we crossed the river and drove another twenty miles before encountering the same scenario—another river to cross, another ferry, another mad dash to get aboard. This time we made it on the first try.

The rest of the trip progressed smoothly . . . until the last five miles. The road suddenly turned into nothing more than a narrow, bumpy dirt path in the middle of vast rice fields. It barely accommodated our car. As darkness grew, we rolled to a halt at a gaping hole in the road. We could not pass.

Nearby villagers hurried around the car and began talking excitedly, bobbing up and down to get a glimpse of the white man inside. I got out my camera to capture the scene and local children screamed with delight after each flash. We stood there for some time making friends, then asked if they would help us fill the hole. Ten minutes later, they returned with shovels. They repaired the road and our trip continued into the night.

When the road ended, friendly villagers greeted us, took my suitcase and materials, and led us down a trail into a small community. To my surprise, we just kept walking, right through that village and on to the next—another mile through the dusty terrain. We finally arrived, completely exhausted, at the home of my host's relative, where we would stay for the five-day seminar.

John's sister-in-law prepared all of our meals outdoors during our visit. I often had little clue what I ate, but I told myself to chew, swallow, and don't ask questions. The food actually tasted quite good. I showered using two buckets of cool water, which felt delightful after the first long, hot, grimy day. My mosquito-netted "bed" consisted of a solid board with several blankets underneath to "soften" it.

Many villagers stayed awake outside our hut late into the first night, talking around kerosene lamps. The village had no electricity or running water. I went to sleep fanning myself but awoke at 1 A.M. to the voices of several men talking loudly outside. I thought I felt an allergy attack coming on, but in my exhaustion I groped around for my trusty earplugs and went back to sleep.

At daybreak, my body grumbled about the hard bed. I simply had to get up. As the day progressed, I came down with a full-blown cold. In all my years of travel, I'd never gotten sick, so never bothered to bring any medicine.

After breakfast, we walked toward a tin building where the seminar would take place. On the way, we heard participants singing loudly in the Bengali language. I recognized several of the praise songs and joined them, singing in English. Believers greeted me warmly and we quickly got into our inductive materials.

By 10 A.M., the sweat poured off me as I taught inside the steaming, small building. It felt like a sauna. My nose dripped constantly, I couldn't stop sneezing, and the long-sleeved white shirt on my back served as my only handkerchief.

Despite my misery, the seminar continued on and the participants appeared to thoroughly enjoy their studies. By 11 A.M. we moved out of the building and continued class under several large shade trees; it felt fifteen degrees cooler.

Between my need to use a translator and the low educational level of the participants—the country had over 25 percent illiteracy rate at that time—the sessions proceeded slowly. Amazingly, after five days of teaching I hadn't lost my voice. Each participant received a certificate and expressed their gratefulness for what they had learned.

The bandits attacked during our last night in the village.

While I slept, six men stationed themselves outside my hut as bodyguards. Sometime during the night, they fell asleep, allowing the bandits to slip into camp. The intruders held guns to the bodyguards' heads and tied them up.

"Which house…American?" the bandits yelled.

The men steadfastly refused to reveal my whereabouts.

The bandits soon threatened to go house-to-house, shedding blood if they did not find me. Tense moments followed. The bandits threatened and screamed at the men, furiously trying to obtain information that would lead to my capture.

"Untie me!" one of the guards finally yelled in an attempt to coax the bandits to let him into his house to get money to pay them off.

In all the commotion, the bandits overlooked one of the six guards, who managed to slip away. He scrambled to several houses in the village, warning families about the renegades.

When one of the guards persuaded a bandit to accompany him to his house for money, he overpowered the would-be robber on the way, dashed inside his house, locked the door, and cried out to his family to

11

sound the alarm. They immediately began banging their tin roof and screaming at the top of their lungs. Their unique version of 911. Soon, I heard the loud ruckus resounding throughout the village.

When the bandits realized the entire village had awakened, they panicked and sprinted off into the night. Within minutes villagers filled our compound, armed with knives and spears. They remained on guard the rest of the night.

As dawn appeared, fifty armed men escorted us out. Potential heavy rains prompted our hosts to move our car to the main highway, so we ended up walking some five miles. After a thirteen-hour trip back to Dhaka, I felt ecstatic to see the pollution — and civilization — of the huge city. I delighted in the clean guesthouse, with its hot showers, air conditioning, and soft bed. On this trip, like so many others, God proved Himself faithful to protect and cover during my journeys to make His word known.

❖ ❖ ❖ ❖ ❖

1
Beginnings

Train up a child in the way he should go,
and when he is old, he will not depart from it.

Proverbs 22:6

I grew up in a Christian home at the base of beautiful San Bernardino Mountains in Mentone, California. My parents, Ross and Mildred Finfrock, ran a farm. Dad owned a chicken operation just down the street from where he grew up. His father, Dr. Ralph Finfrock, moved to Mentone when Dad was just a small boy, along with his sister and three brothers. Grandpa developed about ten acres of naval orange trees in addition to building a successful medical practice.

I began working on the egg ranch at an early age, feeding close to 40,000 chickens both before and after school. I got into organized sports early, I think, in part to get out of feeding those chickens in the afternoon. Dad and Mom, both strong believers, brought my brother, David, two sisters, Susanne and Linda, and me up in the Christian faith. Dad had diabetes and also suffered from arthritis throughout his body, which left him with severely swollen joints and chronic pain, but I rarely heard him complain. He loved the Lord and had a strong faith, praying every morning for the strength to get through another day.

I recall Dad often praying for large sums of money to come in from his egg business so he could provide for our family and keep the business afloat. During family devotions one morning, Dad asked God for $40,000 — and sure enough, within a week the funds came in. He was an extraordinary role model for me, as I watched him live by faith, trusting God to provide. He also gave generously to the churches, missions and to the needy around him.

Dad once confided to me that, years before, he felt God calling him to the mission field, but he never responded. He confessed he always regretted his decision and felt guilty staying home, not serving overseas.

Because of Dad's love for missions, missionaries often stayed in our home. I thought they looked odd in their cultural dress and strange sounding accents. As a teenager, in fact, I considered them social misfits. I thought the best thing to do would be to send them back to whatever country they came from.

I vividly recall wrestling with the Lord one summer about giving my whole life to Him. It happened at Camp Radford in the San Bernardino Mountains, where our church youth group gathered for one week each year. At the end of camp, we always took part in a special fireside service where campers could dedicate their lives to the Lord.

After much soul searching, I finally made a deal with God. I would do anything He wanted me to do, except two things: (1) be a pastor; or (2) be a missionary. So, with those stipulations, I tossed my pinecone into the fire, which confirmed I had dedicated my life to God . . . on my terms, of course.

But God saw my heart's desire.... even if I didn't.
Without either Dad or I am knowing, God was at work, molding, shaping, and preparing one Finfrock for a life in the pastorate and on the mission field — for a life full of adventures in faith.

❖ ❖ ❖ ❖ ❖

2
The Word Comes Alive

So shall My word be that goes forth from my mouth:
It shall not return to Me void, but it shall accomplish what I please,
and it shall prosper in the thing for which I sent it.

Isaiah 55:11

At Redlands High School I excelled in football and baseball, but only average marks as a student. After graduating from high school in 1964 I decided to play both sports at Chaffey Junior College in Southern California. Two successful seasons led to several Universities offering me full scholarships to play football. I ended up choosing the University of Arizona but after one frustrating season the entire coaching staff got fired. It was a bit disappointing even though I got to play before large crowds. I left the university to serve in the Army reserves and a year later I attend Simpson Bible College in San Francisco before transferring to the University of Redlands in Redlands, California in 1969.

Toward the end of my junior year at Redlands, I attended my first meeting of a campus organization called Inter Varsity Christian Fellowship (IVCF). Six girls and one other guy attended the meeting — what a great male/female ratio! When they held elections for the following year's officers, somehow, I found myself elected president and I knew nothing about what I would be presiding over!

15

Our IVCF campus staff adviser, Paul Byer, lived in Pasadena and drove one hour to the Redlands campus to meet with us. Over the years Paul had a tremendous impact upon my life. He asked our leadership team to consider attending a camp the following summer, and when school ended in 1969, we spent a week together in Northern California at the Koinonia Christian Conference Center.

Paul led us in a week-long series of inductive Bible studies. He amazed us all with the insights he helped us glean from the text. He asked questions to get us to observe specific points from the passage and then asked what we thought certain words meant or why we thought the writer wrote what he did. He also challenged us to apply the things we learned. I could not get over the depth or richness of the studies; I'd never experienced the Bible come so alive.

When camp ended, I headed to Mount Hermon Christian Conference Center near Santa Cruz, California, to serve as a camp counselor at Redwood Camp. I fell in love with the place and returned to Mount Hermon each summer for the next five years to work as a staff member.

That first summer I became good friends with the camp's program director, Ron Demolar. The following summer, Mount Hermon opened a beautiful camp for high school students called Ponderosa Lodge; Ron became its director. He asked if I would like to work with him as his program director. I agreed and enjoyed working with some of the finest young people I'd ever met. Summers at the Ponderosa flew by as we ministered to hundreds of young people. Ron continues to be a good friend and currently serves as a board member for ICM.

In the fall of 1969 when the new school year began at Redlands, I could hardly wait to get the IVCF group going. To my dismay, none of the leadership team returned; all of them had dropped out of school. So, I decided to set up the meetings on my own.

I put up signs all around campus explaining the time and place we would meet. When the time came for our first meeting, I arrived late to a room filled to capacity with students. "This must be the wrong room," I said to myself as I sheepishly walked out. "Excuse me," I quizzed a student standing in the hall, "do you know where the IVCF meeting is being held?" He pointed back toward the room I just left.

I began to panic. I expected four, maybe five people to show up, if that. I simply wasn't prepared for a large crowd. I'd planned on having an informal time of sharing and hoped we could discuss what we wanted to do that year. I calmed myself, made my way into the room, and began the meeting. When I described my vision for the campus, others soon chimed in with their ideas. There was a unified sense God wanted to touch the lives of students on our campus. We just needed to tune into His plan.

Paul Byer came to lead us in an inductive Bible study, and everyone began to get excited about the Word. Paul asked a lot of questions about the text, guiding us to analyze it for ourselves. It continued to amaze me how much more alive the Bible seemed to become by using this study technique.

At special weekends we called 'Bible Dig-Ins" we spent hours pouring over various texts—observing, interpreting, and discussing their possible applications. Everyone loved the in-depth studies with Paul. During those days he introduced us to a manuscript study of the Gospel of Mark. He gave us a stack of printed pages containing the biblical text, with no chapter, verse, or paragraph divisions; just page and line numbers. Paul first instructed us read several pages, then go back and put the text in paragraphs. We discussed the conceptual breaks in the text and began noting all the facts within each paragraph. Next, we drew interpretations using the context and made applications as we went along.

Not only did those inductive studies help deepen my biblical understanding, but by using the new study techniques I also began to improve academically in my classes.

During that season a small group of us developed a real passion to pray for revival on campus. Our once a week meeting soon turned into every night prayer meetings in my dorm room. At first, just a few joined us, but before long we packed out the room.

Many an evening, in the middle of the prayer meeting, students reacted as they recognized their sin which separated them from God. Newcomers interrupted our meetings to say, "I don't know what you have, but I want it!" On the spot, we led those students in the sinner's prayer. Over the course of the semester, approximately fifty students came to Christ. Several times we were forced to move to larger quarters when we ran out of space. No one was preaching salvation; no one was teaching. God's power was simply present during those prayer meetings!

Russia

Some twenty-four years later, I again saw God's power transform lives. In 1993 I traveled to Vologda to conduct an Inductive Bible study seminar with a group of pastors and leaders. The middle-aged translator asked to do our seminar taught high school English but had little experience in translating. After the first day of our seminar, I could tell the participants simply were not grasping the concepts.

Our team prayed about the situation — yet the next day our sessions did not improve. I debated canceling the seminar, frustrated because no one understood the content. During the lunch break our translator made a statement which caught my attention. "I hope I will go to heaven someday," she told me. We discussed how she could know for sure she was going to heaven and she eagerly gave her life to Christ, bringing an instant and dynamic transformation to our meetings.

The very next session, for the first time, I saw the pastors and leaders grow attentive. I marveled as God worked through this translator the rest of the week. The Lord now had an open channel through which to work and everyone began to grasp the biblical concepts being taught. Once again, we saw His power displayed.

God's desire is to change lives!

❖ ❖ ❖ ❖ ❖

3
Deep Sorrow And . . . Debbie

He who finds a wife finds a good thing
and obtains favor from the LORD.

Proverbs 18:22

Through a sad, emotional, and even bizarre series of events, the Lord brought my future wife, Debbie, into my life. It all happened during my final year of college at the University of Redlands.

Although my parents lived just three miles from campus, I figured I'd have a lot more fun living in Melrose Hall, a male school dormitory. By working as one of three residence assistants (RAs), I could live there free of charge—a very good thing for a poor college student.

During those days I developed a friendship with Rick, a student whose room was in the dorm basement. He often led worship at our Inter Varsity meetings. I distinctly remember one evening Rick came into my dorm room, excited about a girl he just met at the local YMCA "Upper Room", where a team of Redlands students conducted an outreach ministry. From that night on, week after week, Rick gave me reports about this incredibly beautiful girl. Clearly, he'd fallen head-over-heels in love with her.

One night, Rick came into my room and as usual went on and on about Debbie. "You know," he said, "if this relationship doesn't work out, I know God will help me."

I hadn't really been listening and said something like, "You're right. I'm sure God will help." I didn't know Rick really meant, "If this relationship fails, I won't be able to handle it."

Our conversation was the last time I saw Rick alive. The next morning someone found him hanging from the ceiling of his dorm room.

His suicide stunned me, as it did the entire campus. Police found several notes indicating Rick took his own life because of a broken relationship with Debbie.

I simply needed to find out more about this Debbie. What went wrong? How could Rick have become so desperately depressed? I also thought Debbie could use a friend. I visited the police station to find out where she lived and learned her house was just down the street. In fact, she'd just returned home from a police officer's questioning when I arrived at her front door.

Her mother invited me in. We talked for a few minutes and before Debbie entered the living room. She was indeed beautiful. We talked for a long time and I prayed for her. Before leaving, I asked if I could take her to Rick's funeral. She agreed.

At the funeral, Debbie and I spoke with Rick's parents, a very gracious couple despite their terrible loss. They assured us Debbie was not the cause of Rick's death and he never related well with the opposite sex. He'd had relationships with several other girls in which he fell quickly in love. Because of his strong desire for a serious relationship, the girls all backed away from him. When Debbie told Rick she just wanted to be friends, not boyfriend and girlfriend, Rick saw it as the last straw in series of rejections.

The Most Radical Thing I Could Do

The days following the funeral, I felt sorry for Debbie and went out of my way to spend time with her. I knew she needed Christian fellowship. She'd only recently accepted Christ at a Calvary Chapel beach baptism at Corona Del Mar, California.

Debbie and I began spending more time together. I'd never had a girlfriend, mainly because my coaches drilled it into my head girls and football did not mix. Since my college playing days were coming to an end, I figured it was okay. Our relationship began to blossom.

Three months after our meeting, she and I, along with twenty other students from the Redlands campus, decided to attend an IVCF missionary conference in Urbana, Illinois. It turned out to be an outstanding time, with many excellent speakers, challenging us in the area of missions. One speaker in particular, an African American named Tom Skinner, gave an extremely challenging message.

"What is the most radical thing you can do for Jesus?" Tom asked the crowd, of over eighteen thousand college students from around the world.

I sat there, thinking over and over and over, what radical thing can I do? Suddenly the lights went on. I could ask Debbie to marry me!

Near the very top of the University of Illinois basketball arena after Skinner's challenge, December 1970, I did that very thing. It took her some time to accept my proposal, but eventually we were on our way.

On April 3, 1971, shortly before I graduated, Pastor Chuck Smith from Calvary Chapel Costa Mesa drove out to the Redlands First Baptist Church to officiate at our wedding. I'd become acquainted with Pastor Chuck two years earlier when he came out to teach our IVCF group in Redlands. I loved his teaching and, since Debbie was born again through his ministry, we wanted Pastor Chuck to marry us.

About two months prior to our marriage, I began having serious doubts whether we should marry at all. Maybe my doubts came from never having seriously dated anyone before. I came into the relationship with little understanding of the opposite sex or of the differences between how males and females operate, plus we'd received no pre-martial counseling. At age twenty-six, I had no clue what I was getting into and I feared I might be making the wrong choice.

Ultimately, God's grace covered our naivety. As a pastor some forty-eight years later, I would never consider marrying a couple who hadn't undergone at least eight pre-marital counseling sessions.

Before the wedding, I worried about Debbie's non-Christian background and family life. She came from an extremely articulate family. Her father, a colonel in the Air Force, held a doctorate in education and the family participated in intense, intellectual discussions on a myriad of topics. As a teenager, Debbie got caught in the middle of an all-out domestic war. A divorce ultimately left her home broken and her family in pieces. In the fallout she embraced the sixties hippy culture of peace, love, and transcendental meditation.

My family had its own challenges. While we loved each other very much, we communicated poorly. We rarely discussed issues or concerns. And when we disagreed, we didn't express our thoughts or feelings. We just kept them inside. I wish I'd seen constructive conflict resolution modeled in my home.

So, as I contemplated marriage, I decided to lay a "fleece" before the Lord, much like Gideon did in the Bible when he was about to go to war (Judges 6). I knew Pastor Chuck's ministry had grown rapidly and he was extremely busy. I said to the Lord, "If Debbie and I can get into see Chuck right away, and if he agrees to come to Redlands to marry us, then I know I'm supposed to marry this women." As unrealistic as it may sound, God took me at my word.

When we called Pastor Chuck, he invited us to see him right away. As we talked in his office, he agreed to come to Redlands for the wedding. When we walked out of his office, I knew in my heart, Okay Lord, I get it, you want me to marry this woman!

A Long, Hard Road

Little did Debbie and I know, but we were in for a long, hard road together. Perhaps our honeymoon should have foreshadowed what lay ahead.

Debbie developed female problems the second night after the wedding and ended up in the hospital for one week. Instead of coming away from the honeymoon with our hearts joined in romantic union, we came away with an enormous hospital bill which started off our marriage in staggering debt.

As I'd feared, the negatives from Debbie's background and mine collided and led to a few turbulent years. Debbie always wanted to talk and probe about different topics or relational issues, while I chose to avoid them like the plague. I also became so deeply involved in ministry and coaching football; I often used the excuse I felt "too tired" to talk. These conflicts—all of which seemed "minor" at first—ultimately snowballed and became major challenges in the years to follow.

One month after our wedding we headed to Northern California to Mount Hermon to work as summer staff. I worked there for the past five summers and brought my new bride to Ponderosa Lodge where I enjoyed many returning friends, wonderful memories, and a stimulating job working as program director. Debbie, on the other hand, had no friends and an unexciting job as camp secretary. We found little if any time to develop our relationship—everything centered on ministry. Looking back, I can see the dangerous trappings of it all.

While I enjoyed every minute of my work, Debbie struggled. When the summer ended, we flew to Michigan for Inter Varsity staff training. Once again, we allowed ministry to dominate our relationship. We became like two strangers living together. I now understand why Old Testament warriors often got a whole year off when they married. It gave them time to develop a relationship which would endure the years to come, including times of hardship and separation. Despite our initial poor relationship and with the help of wise counsel, God faithfully kept us together.

Working With IVCF

In the spring of 1971, I earned my college degree. I crammed four years of college into six, but I made it. Although I often struggled in the classroom, I somehow earned a "B" average.

After graduation, Paul Byer talked to me about becoming a staff intern with Inter Varsity. Prior to his offer, I thought God might be leading me into teaching and coaching football. Already in 1970, I coached football, basketball, and baseball at Redlands High School, and I relished every minute of it. I'd even started a Bible study with some athletes and was given the privilege of leading young men to the Lord.

But the possibility of working with Paul and IVCF intrigued me. When I prayed about this new opportunity I said, "Father, I thought you wanted me to be a coach?"

I sensed His gentle reply, "I am calling you to be a coach . . . but in a much broader sense. You'll see."

❖ ❖ ❖ ❖ ❖

4
Lessons of Faith 101

For we walk by faith,
not by sight.

2 Corinthians 5:7

God gives us experiences and lessons early in life as building blocks for faith. The promise I'd made to God as a teenager at camp—when I vowed to dedicate my life to Him so long as He wouldn't ask me to become a missionary or pastor—backfired.

For six years I ministered full-time with Inter Varsity. Although Debbie was a young believer, she immediately got thrust into the role of spiritual counselor and leader with the girls on campus. In fact, she had no clue how to offer biblical counsel to anyone. She also was still trying to figure out what she'd gotten herself into by marrying me!

Through IVCF I not only got a good taste of teaching Inductive Bible Studies, I also got to fulfill another passion: Coaching.

In my second year on staff with IVCF, in 1973, I ran into my former football coach, Frank Serrao, a man of integrity whom I greatly respected and admired. I enjoyed a successful football career, playing tackle and linebacker under Frank's capable leadership, and was thrilled when he asked if I would join his football coaching staff at the University of Redlands.

For the next four years IVCF ministry and football consumed my time. Debbie and I invited players over for meals, followed by a Bible study — and they ate it all up literally and spiritually. They absolutely loved Debbie's cooking and before long thirty plus players were showing up for dinner. We almost went broke feeding them, but the Bible studies yielded rich rewards. Again, I was given the opportunity of leading many of those young men to Christ.

Several of our players mentioned the Bible study to a reporter for the San Bernardino Sun Telegram, who covered our games. One day she caught me after practice and asked if she could attend a study. Although I felt a bit reluctant, for fear of what kind of spin she would put in her article, I agreed to let her join us.

Two days later, the top headline on the front page of the sports section read: "Christ Helps U of R Football Players!" To our pleasant surprise, the reporter penned a remarkably positive story about how many of our players attributed our success to Christ's presence in their lives.

Life as a Pastor

In 1978 I took my first church pastorate in Redlands.

I worked as an assistant at a small fellowship . . . but not for long. After just six months, the church "split" over the issue of water baptism. More than three-quarters of the congregation left and planted a new church. We helped out at the new church, but not in an official capacity.

Several months later a door opened for us to move to Austin, Texas, to help start what would become Austin Christian Fellowship. The pastor, Dr. Bill Rodgers, asked if I would assist. I knew Dr. Rodgers and his family from the Christian and Missionary Alliance church where I grew up. I agreed to help, without salary, and to support my family I worked a construction job.

Debbie must have wondered what on earth I was thinking, working construction all day and taking on another ministry responsibility with no pay. After all, it wasn't just the two of us anymore. In the span of four years, Debbie gave birth to three Finfrock children: Lela Marie, born in 1974; Corrie Jean, in 1975; and Nathan Daniel, in 1977. We almost lost Nathan at birth, due to a collapsed lung, but after ten days in ICU and much prayer, he pulled through.

During our time in Austin, God gave me an incredible hunger for His Word. I often got up in the wee hours of the morning to spend time reading His Word and meditating upon it. After breakfast, I headed off to work for ten hours of physical labor. By the end of the day I felt exhausted, but I always tried to spend some time with my family before going to bed. During our stay in Texas, God taught us many lessons, often painful, about blind faith and complete trust.

We learned one of our early lessons in obedient faith during the winter of 1978. It rained for two consecutive weeks, drenching construction sites and making it impossible to work. We ran out of money and, to compound our problems, our home in Redlands kept falling out of escrow during three separate attempts to sell it. We maxed out our credit cards and couldn't make payments. It got so bad at one point we ran out of food.

Twice I picked up the phone to call my parents, who I knew would send money if I explained our dire straits. But both times it seemed as if God was on the other end. I heard His words in my mind, almost as if He whispered them verbally: "Don't you dare call your parents, Dan. Trust Me!" Reluctantly, I set the phone down and obeyed the Lord.

Daily I went to the mailbox, almost ritualistically, to see if anyone might have sent us money. As I looked in the mailbox one day, I heard His voice again in my head saying, "Why are you looking in here? I will provide for you. Trust Me!"

The next morning, we had no food in the house and no money to purchase anything. I got up early, praying and seeking God. The kids walked into the kitchen, wondering what was for breakfast. Instead of eating, we gathered around the dining room table and prayed. As I began to pray, I also began to cry. The children sensed something was wrong, since they rarely saw Daddy in tears.

Moments later, at 8 A.M., we heard a knock at the front door. As I opened the door Pastor Bill's wife, Iva, stood there with two grocery bags of food. I invited her in, and she explained that during the night she had an unexplainable nudge to go out early in the morning and bring us groceries. She almost apologized because she didn't know whether she heard the directions correctly.

God once again proved Himself faithful to meet our needs. What a lesson for Debbie and I and especially for the children!

During this season of learning trust and obedience, Debbie and I decided not use credit cards any longer. We cut up all of our cards except for one I kept secretly hidden in my wallet (in case of an emergency).

As I drove home from work one evening, the gas gauge needle pushed toward empty. I knew I needed to get to work the next day and my daughter, Lela, needed to get to her school—but how could I pay for gas? I'd not used my credit card in weeks. I rationalized I could use the credit card just this time. I didn't know if Debbie would agree, but I needed to get to work the following morning.

I pulled into a gas station, filled the tank with a few gallons, and headed home. The closer I got, the guiltier I felt. By the time I arrived, I felt totally convinced I should confess to Debbie I'd secretly kept a credit card and just used it for gas. Once inside, I spilled my guts and asked her and the Lord to forgive me. I cut up the last credit card and went to bed.

I woke up the next day to rain, which meant no work for me. Not only that, but a holiday at my daughter's school meant she didn't need to go. Sure enough, there was no need for me to put gas in the car the evening before.

The following day money was provided to meet our needs and once again I learned some hard lessons in trusting Him. More lessons followed during the months ahead — precious lessons, yet painful. Little did we know He was preparing us for a much bigger faith venture which would take us around the world.

Feeding of the 5000 — Minus 4,800

Years later when we lived in the Philippines, the Lord built upon those early lessons of faith learned in Texas. I was getting ready to visit another island to conduct an Inductive Bible Study seminar with about 200 pastors, when my director of finances informed me, we did not have enough money to do the seminar. We had funds for only one day's food supply, when we scheduled a four-day event. Our ministry normally provided two meals per day and helped with transportation costs for out-of-town pastors. My colleague thought we should cancel the seminar.

I gathered the rest of my staff together and described the situation. We prayed and sought the Lord together. After some time, we agreed not to cancel the seminar, trusting God would provide.

Our team left for the seminar location and gave the cook all the money we had for food. At the marketplace he purchased a large quantity of food, which prompted a lot of people to ask, "Why are you buying so much?" He told them, that about 200 pastors were coming from all over the islands to participate in our seminar. The vendors were so touched they asked if they could donate more rice and vegetables. Our cook came back with an abundance of food which lasted all four days! God once again proved Himself faithful.

❖ ❖ ❖ ❖ ❖

5
I Will Do A New Thing . . .

Behold I will do a new thing,
now it shall spring forth...

Isaiah 43: 19

As the months went by, the church in Austin was struggling and I had some differences with the pastor's leadership style. I began to feel uneasy about staying much longer.

One day I got into my car and drove out to a desolate area for a day of prayer and fasting, seeking direction. I picked a flat area full of sweet-smelling pines and found a fallen tree where I could sit and began reading the Word.

A text in Isaiah grabbed my attention. I meditated on His words, drinking them in: *"Do not remember the former things nor consider the things of old. Behold I will do a new thing, now it shall spring forth; shall you not know it? I will even make a road in the wilderness and rivers in the desert"* (Isaiah 43: 18, 19).

I looked down from my Bible and right next to me, at my feet, grew a tiny pine tree. As sure as I write today, I felt the Lord speaking to my heart: "As I am bringing new life in this little tree, so I am bringing new life into you. Watch and see, as I bring forth something brand new from your life." I drove home completely uplifted and encouraged.

As Debbie and I continued to pray for direction, we both had a strong desire to reconnect with Calvary Chapel. Chuck Smith impressed us during our Inter Varsity days with his teaching and understanding of the Bible. God used Pastor Chuck in a powerful way as he led thousands to Christ at the beginning of the Jesus Movement in the late 1960s and early 1970s. Both Debbie and I saw Calvary Chapel as the place for us to get involved.

In the Spring, of 1978 we moved back to Redlands, California, intending to start a Calvary Chapel in the area. It did not faze us several attempts to start a Calvary in Redlands failed. God was doing a "new thing" and I felt positive He called us back to Redlands to do that very thing.

Shortly after our move back, I discovered Pastor Don McClure recently started a Calvary Chapel in Redlands. A cloud of disappointment and confusion settled over me. How could I have so misread God's will, especially when sensing such specific direction?

I met with Pastor Don while he was laying sod in his front yard and in a few minutes, he recruited me to help. After a long talk and a lot of sweat, he invited me to join forces with the new church plant. Since no other opportunity for service presented itself, I accepted the invitation and began working with the youth and helping out as much as I could while holding down a job delivering eggs. Although I disliked driving a truck, the job provided me with lots of time to listen to tapes and grow in my faith while driving routes.

A New Work in Banning

I met Ken Kienow, an elder at Calvary Chapel Redlands, during the first year back in Redlands. Ken just started a ministry focusing on evangelistic outreach called Intensive Care Ministries. He invited me to become a board member and soon we started doing musical concert outreach events throughout the area.

We held some concerts in the nearby City of Banning in an open-air amphitheater, where we saw many lives changed in exciting ways. All the positive things happening prompted us to contact the city's churches to make known our desire to channel new believers into their fellowships. We got no response from any of them, and with no place to send all the new believers, we decided to start a Bible study in Cherry Valley, at the home of Steve and Kathy Higgins, just five minutes from Banning.

The members of the Bible study, many of whom drove thirty miles to church in Redlands, began expressing a desire to start a Calvary Chapel in Banning. After some time, Debbie and I decided to begin this new work.
Don McClure gave us his blessing, helped us get started, and in late 1979 Calvary Chapel Banning began meeting in the Banning Community Center. Each Sunday we arrived at the center early to pick up beer and wine bottles scattered in the parking lot and to set up for the service. Although the stench of alcohol often permeated the meeting room, we broke out heavy duty cleaners and got the place looking and smelling fresh before each service.

A year after starting the church, we rented a home in the Banning community and moved our family. We enrolled our children in local schools, where they were a minority due to the large numbers of African Americans, Hispanics, and Laotians. Slowly the church grew and gained momentum.

Banning's economy was weak in the 80's and many minorities lived within the city limits. Eventually the government moved hundreds of Laotian refugees into the area. We began an outreach to Laotian refugees and created a food ministry, giving away a great deal of food to families throughout the community. One family in our church even donated several acres of land on which we invited the refuges to farm, free of charge. Many of the refugees farmed in their home countries and were thrilled to take advantage of our offer. To irrigate the land our people channeled water from the mountains into a large reservoir. It worked ideally until one night the dirt wall broke and flooded most of the crops. Gophers had weakened the walls with their digging. With a little ingenuity, we worked out another watering system and the gardens flourished again, giving many refugee's provisions and family income.

I look back at that time of working the soil and sweating side-by-side with refugees as a remarkable season during which we shared Christ in word and deed. He not only worked and ministered faithfully among those precious refugees, but also among us His church body.

More adventures in faith awaited us.

❖ ❖ ❖ ❖ ❖

6
From Football Field to Mission Field

*Call unto Me, and I will answer you, and show you
great and mighty things, which you do not know.*

Jeremiah 33:3

Our first worship leader at Calvary Chapel of Banning in 1982 was
Dennis McGee who worked at a reform school for boys called Twin
Pines located about 30 miles from our home. The young men at Twin
Pines came out of prison and were required to live at the school before
their permanent release. They attended high school, and many
competed in sports with nearby public and private schools.

When Dennis heard of my coaching experience, he asked if I would help
their new head football coach. I couldn't resist the opportunity and soon
went to work as Coach Lou Haden's assistant.

When we began working with these young men, I discovered many
were getting into trouble off the field. They had committed a laundry
list of crimes, from car theft to drug dealing, and it showed — I could
sense the anger bottled up inside them.

At one of our first practices, I told the boys I didn't want to hear any
more foul language. Some made admirable attempts to stop cussing, but

I soon realized those tough kids found it next to impossible to talk without using expletives. I'd never heard so much filthy language, but as time went on, it tapered off. They also quickly learned cussing out a referee gets you kicked out of the game. That helped my cause!

We were entrusted with some remarkable, raw talent and ended the first season undefeated. I think those boys used the football field as a place to vent their frustrations. They often pleaded with Coach Lou and I to let them "go live" during practice which meant they could hit hard, despite rock hard dirt fields. They just loved to slam each other as aggressively as they could. In one game our players hit the opponents so hard, after halftime the opposing team refused to come back out to play.

Midway through the season, I started a Bible study with players and eventually several committed their lives to Christ. Slowly, I saw some of those hardened, hurting boys soften.

So did one of their coaches.

One day as we rode the bus home from an away game, Coach Haden and I talked about the game. Somehow, the conversation turned to what it meant to be a Christian. Eventually I asked Lou if he ever committed his life to Jesus Christ.

"No, I haven't," he said.

We talked more about football and the boys, but I sensed Lou was mulling over our discussion about following Christ.

"Lou," I said, "would you like to pray with me to receive Christ into your life?"

Right there on the old school bus, Lou invited Jesus into his heart. As the bus barreled down the freeway, I could almost hear angels rejoicing!

I would later find out Lou's wife, Peggy, had been praying for years for her husband to become born-again.

From Football to . . . Women's Aglow?

Some ladies in my church asked me in 1982 to serve as an adviser for their Women's Aglow group, an international outreach to women with a local chapter in Banning. Halfheartedly I agreed and periodically began attending their meetings. At one meeting someone spoke a clear, concise, prophetic word about my future.

Debbie's cousin, Phyllis Atadero, served as the main speaker. She'd done a fine job leading the ladies in a Bible study. At the end of the session, Phyllis turned to her husband, an ordained minister. "Andy," she said, "do you have anything to say?"

Andy stood without hesitating and announced, "I have a word from the Lord—for Dan."

As the only other male in a room of more than 100 ladies, I felt conspicuous. He asked me to stand and reluctantly I obeyed. Although I turned ten shades of red, Andy boldly spoke, God was going to use me in a ministry which would take me around the globe. He called it a critical end-time's ministry.

I felt taken back. Before I knew it, he started praying for me. I left the Aglow meeting in a daze, pondering the words Andy predicted about the future.

As I reflect on these words, many years later, I have seen this prophesy fulfilled. We have taught the Inductive Bible Study in more than fifty-three countries, translated training materials into more than fifty languages, and established directors in Africa, South America, India, Pakistan and the Philippines.

I also see this prophecy as a confirmation of the word I received in Austin, Texas as I sat on a fallen log, "I will do something new."

Not long after Andy's prophecy, I began receiving letters from a Filipino pastor named Benito Pacleb, asking me to come to the Philippines. After some investigating, I learned Benito had about 40 Filipino pastors under his ministry. I also found out one of my good friends, Pastor Roger Scalice from Calvary Chapel in Everett, Washington, also received letters from Benito inviting him to visit. Together, Roger and I committed to go to the Philippines, but some issues came up in my church which forced me to pull out.

Roger went by himself and came back excited about what he'd seen and heard. He enjoyed many opportunities to minister and saw a great need, especially for the teaching of the Word among the Filipino pastors. In time, the Lord began to stir Roger's heart to move to the Philippines to plant a Calvary Chapel in Manila.

Finally, I'm Off!

Roger planned a trip back to the Philippines in 1983. I came up with my own funds to accompany him. I'd only traveled a little during my football days with University of Arizona, so I felt excited about my first overseas trip. I guess I thought we would hop on a jet and just "be there."

How wrong I was.

After a flight of sixteen hours, it seemed to take forever to crawl through the long lines in customs. A swarm of taxi drivers practically accosted us; one of them whisked us less than a mile to the domestic terminal, at an inflated rate of $20.

Lesson learned.

Hours later we finally boarded our connecting flight to Dumaguete City in the southern islands of the Philippines. After one hour in the air, the plane circled the airport and made a dramatic landing — touching down, brakes screeching, rolling toward the ocean, and coming to rest just twenty yards short of the choppy sea. Later I learned the airport's runway was one of the shortest in the region.

A friend shared, "Once in a while, planes just can't stop in time."

Pastor Pacleb, several of his pastors, and people from his church warmly greeted Roger and I with leis. We climbed into his vehicle and headed down the coast to the conference center. Motorcycles pulling small cabs known as peticabs — which could comfortably carry one large American, or about four Filipinos — crammed the narrow roads.

The conference site stood right on the beach and we gathered with more than 100 pastors in a tiny building with a rusty tin roof. I will never forget the hunger of those pastors for God's Word. They took out their Bibles, scooted forward in their chairs, organize their papers and pens, and eagerly awaited the teaching.

After teaching about forty-five minutes, I began wrapping up my lesson in Ephesians when I noticed something very unusual. Unlike at my home church, I did not see the tired eyes and antsy body language of people in a hurry to get home. Not one pastor as much as glanced at his watch. No one looked around the room with bored expressions. And even though the temperature must have been pushing 90 degrees in the hot humid tin building, not one pastor nodded off.

As I began my concluding remarks, Benito urged me, "Please, Brother Dan, do not stop your study. It is very good! Please, could you keep going?" In all my years of pastoring, no one ever asked me to extend a sermon!

41

On the contrary, some in my church wished I would have stopped sooner.

During our breaks, pastors told Roger and I they never heard the Bible taught verse-by-verse. Our simple, expository teaching of God's Word was revolutionary to them. They knew of topical studies only. They had limited, if any, training on how to take apart a Biblical text inductively. God was showing me the tremendous, glaring need for solid Bible teaching.

After two weeks of conferences, Roger and I headed back to the States. Roger returned more certain than ever God was directing him to start a church in Manila, and so he began finalizing his plans. I headed back to my church and remember becoming irritated with my congregation as individuals once again began giving me the "signals" when they felt I should wrap up the sermon. I was so frustrated I wanted to beat them over the head with my Bible. They didn't realize pastors in the Philippines were starving for what they felt so anxious to discard. Many didn't understand the incomprehensible gift God has granted us—to study His Word, in-depth, week after week.

Over the next few months, letters arrived from many pastors who attended our conference. Not only did they thank me, but they invited me to come back the following year. After much prayer, I agreed to return. But this time, I would not go alone. I would take two board members from our church with me. Together, we would see the hunger for God's Word.

Change of Heart

The first time I traveled to Manila, members of our church said things like, "Manila? Why are you going all the way over there? Our church has enough problems of its own. Don't you think you should stay home and take care of the needs here?"

The second time around, they had a change of heart. In fact, they pitched in on a work project and raised funds for my travel and two of our board members!

Roger, who already moved to the Philippines with his family, met the three of us at the airport and took us to his home for several days before we headed to Dumaguete City. We enjoyed a refreshing time with old friends.
Once in the southern islands, we received another warm welcome and soon got underway with our teaching. As I spoke one night the Lord flashed a clear, distinct image in my mind, one which ultimately would change the direction of our lives.

In just a few seconds, I saw all the listening Filipino pastors on one side of the room and a married couple I recognized from my church on the other side. This couple had come to me just prior to my departure, confiding to me the words every pastor loves to hear: "Pastor, we are going to be leaving the church because we are just not being fed here." In this vivid picture in my mind, I saw the couple sitting, completely bloated, as if someone had taken an air compressor and pumped them up to the exploding point.

On the other side of the room sat all the local pastors we came to teach, whom I pictured as skin and bones. "This is a picture of my church," God distinctly showed me. "In America the church is bloated because it has so much available. But my church in the Third World is starving for my Word. I want you to leave your church, Dan, and invest your life into Third World pastors—teach them how to study my Word."

As the conference concluded, I realized my season as pastor of Calvary Chapel of Banning was coming to an end. Beyond a shadow of a doubt, I knew God was directing us to leave our church and move to the Philippine. But as I flew home, I couldn't get rid of a nagging question: How would Debbie and our three children respond to this new opportunity? Would Debbie think I lost my mind? Would the kids commit mutiny? What would the congregation think when they heard I intended to step down? Would they feel happy? Sad? Angry?

To my relief and pleasant surprise, Debbie responded with an openness to consider this new venture. Although she did not feel any strong personal calling, she would wait on the Lord to confirm the move.

In order to avoid making such a critical decision on a solitary person's convictions, Debbie and I agreed to first receive individual confirmation from the Lord. If both of us agreed God was directing us to go, then we would have no room for pointing fingers later if problems arose or times got rough. Secondly, we sought counsel from a couple mission organizations and respected friends. Most of the congregation expressed a positive reaction. The board stood behind us 100 percent and committed to back us financially, a pleasant surprise. The children all viewed the move as a great adventure and were excited about moving across the world. In fact, one door after another opened and by January of 1985, we got ready to hit the road.

The church agreed to supply us with a monthly salary for a specific time, but we would have to trust the Lord for the funds needed to purchase our airfare and get some of our things moved overseas. Several mission agencies told us we would need about $10,000 to make the move. We prayed for the funds and some came in, but nothing close to the suggested amount.

Two weeks before our departure date, we collected just enough money to buy each person in our family a one-way ticket. Then, one week before our planned exodus, another $3,000 came in for our move — far short of the $10,000 we prayed for, but God continued to assure us to trust Him. We packed all we could into two suitcases each and chose not to ship any of our things. Beyond that, we gave virtually everything away, determined to get to the Philippines. We wanted to live in the southern islands, specifically in Dumaguete City where I previously visited. When we arrived, we spent the first week in a hotel, but knew we couldn't stay very long before our money ran out. That's when we asked Pastor Benito Pacleb, who hosted the pastors' conferences the previous two years, if he could help us find a home.

In a most generous act of hospitality, Pastor Benito and his wife, June, opened their home to us. For the next three weeks, their three boys and our three kids and the adults all crowded into that small house—ten bodies in two bedrooms, all using one small bathroom.
It gave us the enriching opportunity to experience the hospitality and graciousness of our new Filipino friends.

A Surprising Home and a Leaky Car

People with experience living in the Philippines told us not to expect much when looking for living quarters. They called it "next to impossible" to find a rental home with furnishings. Debbie and I had visions of a small hut with dirt floors and a thatched roof.

Amazingly, five weeks into our transition, we came across a house located near the beach—and we could afford it! The fairly new house stood within a large compound owned by a wealthy Spanish family. It came with three bedrooms and a servant's quarters, each having its own bathroom. It boasted a dining room, a living room, and a kitchen, and the place came completely furnished for—get this—$150 per month, with two months advance rent required. Thrilled, we thanked God for His provision.

Next, I set my sights on finding a reliable car; but once again, it wouldn't be easy. It was necessary to search hard to find a vehicle. The area had no newspaper ads or rental magazines, so you needed to know someone who knew someone who knew someone else who wanted to sell a car.

A new friend we made through Pastor Pacleb's church, Larry Montenegro, turned out to be just the man we needed. As a successful businessman, he knew how to wheel and deal. Larry took me to the next island, Cebu, where he heard of a vehicle for sale.

No one would call the Filipino-made Pinoy the most beautiful vehicle ever driven off the assembly line, but this practical car could carry ten people! None of the windows had glass except the windshield, and only one wiper worked—sometimes. Whenever it rained, a frequent occurrence, we dropped a bunch of plastic flaps to keep from getting soaked.

Larry haggled the owner from $3,000 down to $1,500; before he finished, he had the owner feeling guilty he charged us even that much!

God multiplied our limited resources. We were learning to trust Him for all our needs.

❖ ❖ ❖ ❖ ❖

7

Unto Us A Son Is Given

I will not leave you orphans;
I will come to you.

John 14:18

At the end of March 1985, we received an eye-opening letter from a board member at our home church. Financial difficulties meant they would have to significantly reduce our support.

I was taken back by this sudden turn of events. Several questions loomed. How would we support ourselves? Had we heard God right when we made the move? Doubt slowly crept in. This adventure of faith was not so easy! I needed to learn trusting God involves making determined choices. We could either give in to fear or choose to trust His Word. During this period of struggle, I paid a visit to Pastor Pacleb, who lived just outside the city.

On the way, I noticed a woman standing on the side of the road with a baby in her arms. I didn't think much about it as I drove on with two of our children, Corrie and Nathan. After an hour or more of visiting with Benito and June, the children and I headed back home.

The same lady was still standing alongside the road but this time her face looked filled with anxiety. I pulled over and asked if she needed a ride into town. She nodded and climbed in with the baby.

Without prompting, she began crying as she told us the story of the tiny baby boy cradled in her arms. The birth mother of the three-week-old died of malnutrition shortly after childbirth. The father, a blind beggar, lived in a town many miles away and could not care for him. The authorities gave the baby to his maternal grandmother, now in her eighties also who was unable to properly care for him. The baby became sick and weak; the grandmother knew the baby would die.

Because of local superstition, the grandmother begged this woman, whom she did not know, to take the baby so it would not die in her home. Many Filipinos fear the spirit of death, which they believe will return to haunt those left behind.

I asked the woman where she needed to go. She requested to be taken to her pastor's home. When we arrived, the man opened the door and listened to the newborn's plight, but he could offer no help.

The women got back into the car with tears said this baby is dying. He needed hospital care, but she had no money. I knew I could no longer remain a bystander. I dropped the lady off in town and kept the baby. Arriving home, I honked the horn. Debbie came out.

"Guess what I've brought home!"

We took the baby inside and unwrapped him for the first time.

He was pathetically thin—less than five pounds and severely dehydrated. We knew he didn't have much time left.

Debbie and I rushed him to the hospital. After several doctors examined him, they told us he would likely die. They suggested if we wanted to buy some medicine, they would do their best to keep him alive. I hurried out, purchased the medicine, and we stayed at the hospital with the baby.

For the next ten days, the tiny guy hovered between life and death. Debbie and our two helpers rotated shifts to be at his bedside praying and being available for any needed assistance. To our amazement and the doctors and nurses, this little fighter would not give in to death. Around the tenth day, he began to make an unexpected recovery. Debbie began asking what would happen to him once he was discharged. A government worker told us he would be sent to an orphanage. She inquired if we could keep him.

The worker responded, not only could we keep him, but plenty more were available if we wanted them!

After a couple of months caring for him in our home, we fell in love with this little guy whom we named Aaron. We began to question the Lord, "What should we do? Do You want us to keep him as foster parents?" He still was experiencing some health issues, along with allergies which kept him from taking normal milk products. It would be very expensive to feed him, more than an average Filipino family made in one month (about $50). We knew he would have little chance of surviving in an orphanage set up for healthy babies and children.

Next, we brought our children into the discussion. We asked each one if they had any problem adding Aaron to our family. The unanimous vote: Keep him!

We told the social worker we wanted him and filled out the paperwork to become foster parents. After several weeks we needed to decide whether or not to keep him permanently. By this time, he owned our hearts! We continued to pray, asking God what to do. He responded by speaking into my thoughts with a tender small voice.

"Dan, you are to keep this little boy. He will be a sign to you of what I have called you to do. As you look at this little boy, you see he is weak and frail. That is the condition of many of my churches in the Philippines. As you take the baby boy into your home, feeding and nourishing him, he will grow and become strong—and so will My church as it learns to feed upon My Word. I've brought you here to teach these pastors how to study My Word and teach it to others."

Despite our discouragement about finances, God confirmed our calling by giving us this little boy, whom we named Aaron Omay (pronounced "Oh My!") Finfrock. The Aaron of the Bible helped his brother Moses, and our Aaron would become a helper and a sign to us. We chose his Filipino last name as his middle name. Many times, we would proclaim, "Oh my, what have we done?"

Soon, Aaron became the center of our affection. What a character he turned out to be, full of what my mother would have called "vim and vinegar." He hit the ground running each day and didn't stop until well past dark. As soon as his dark little head hit the pillow, he was out to the world. It took a year to finalize the adoption, but by age two Aaron became an official Finfrock.

The doctors watched Aaron's progress closely over the next few years. They informed us he might suffer from a mental handicap, because of his rough start in life. Some of his baby teeth came in hollow due to poor prenatal nutrition. During a brief furlough when Aaron was about four, a close dentist friend in the States spent hours filling Aaron's teeth in an attempt to keep them from breaking apart. Aaron sat in my lap, sometimes falling asleep, as Dr. Hank Mercado gently worked on him. Though Dr. Hank spent so much time on Aaron, he refused to charge us.

From day one, Debbie filled up Aaron with lots of vitamins, plenty of nourishing food, and loads of tender, loving care. We watched him grow and become healthy. Despite some learning disabilities which hindered him in school, he got along just fine.

Aaron Grows & God Provides

In our first year with Aaron, God began providing for us financially in unexpected ways. When I went to the post office to get our mail, I often noticed some of our mail had been opened, no doubt looking for money. But several times in unopened letters, we found checks for $1,000. We had no clue who sent us the money, but we saw God provide for us time and time again.

I invited a number of pastor friends from the States to visit and do seminars with me. The work intrigued them. They saw immense value in it and became solid supporters. Slowly, God built a support network for our ministry, enabling us to rent office space and hold two to three seminars a month. Their excitement and support encouraged me to create an Inductive Bible Study training course designed to meet the specific needs of Filipino pastors.

At first when I began to travel to different islands, I did not tell how our family found and adopted Aaron. But soon I began to conclude the seminars by telling his story and message the Lord had given me regarding his life. I also shared the Filipino church needed systematic Bible teaching of God's Word. During the next six years, I gave the same testimony to thousands of pastors and never once did any disagree the church in the Philippines (at that time) needed more Biblical teaching. Instead, they continuously confirmed the truth which came forth through Aaron's life. Today the bible is being taught systematically in various independent and denominational churches all over the Philippines.

We experienced many fun moments with Aaron as part of our family. It didn't take long for the Filipinos to notice him and accept us into the community because of what we'd done for him. Sometimes I would walk down the street, holding Aaron, and someone would come up and say, "Is that your son?"

"Yes, this is my son,"
"Are you married to a Filipina?" they would ask.
"No, I'm not."

They would walk away, puzzled.

When Debbie and I were together with Aaron, people would say, "He is so dark, and you are so white. Why?"

We would tease them and say, "When you have a child in a country, it comes out the color of the people in the country...don't you know?" Often it took a moment for the joke to sink in, but when realized, they would always laugh.

Aaron loved being perched on my shoulders as we walked around town. One day we visited a gymnasium packed with 1,000 people attending a school event which involved our girls, and we could find no place to sit. Aaron sat on my shoulders as I stood near the gym floor. The rambunctious little guy launched backward without warning and slammed his head against my back. Because he did this a lot, I had grown used to it, holding his legs so he wouldn't fly off. An enormous, "Ohhh" escaped from the crowd expecting disaster. I looked around to see what caused the excitement and realized everyone was staring at us. Surprise! It was just Aaron, now sitting straight up and beaming from ear to ear.

One day when Aaron was about three our family drove down a dirt road. He leaned out the back window, as he often did, to let the wind cool him off. Our car had no seat belts, so someone always hung on to him, but on this occasion, we failed to pay attention. He accidentally bumped the side door latch and tumbled out of the moving car.

Debbie let out a piercing scream and I slammed on the brakes.

We jumped out and dashed back to him. Aaron looked stunned, but when he saw the panic on our faces, he burst out crying. Fortunately, except for a few scratches, he came through it unscathed. We shook our heads in wonder.

Oh my, I thought, what must God have in store for this young boy?

Rumors & Rescue

As teaching opportunities increased, I began hearing a nasty rumor. A woman in town apparently had begun visiting all of the local churches, spreading the lie our family adopted Aaron for the sole purpose of raising money in the States. For a season, people told me this story at virtually every church I visited. I felt furious and began defending our family.

But God told me to stop it. He assured me He would deal with this woman.

So, what did He want me to do?

"Pray for her. Forgive her for the harm she's done to you. And don't defend yourself."

I found this difficult at first. But over time, I knew if I clung to the anger, it would eventually consume me and make me completely ineffective. After some time, the issue just slipped away. We never heard another word about it.

I have came to realize all of us have much in common with our son, Aaron. We had no hope and no future until Jesus Christ appeared to rescue us. Doctors told us if we hadn't brought Aaron in when we did, he would not have survived. The same is true of us. If Christ never came, we would be dead in our sins. He did come to rescue each of us, adopt us into His family, and make us His personal heirs.

What an unfathomable privilege to be part of the family of God!

When people asked Aaron, "What is your name?" he always responded, "My name is Aaron Finfrock." He didn't look like a Finfrock, but because we adopted him into our family, he became a joint heir with his brother and two sisters. He became the child of parents who vowed to love him unconditionally, forever.

As we believe in Christ's birth, His life, death, and resurrection, we are the most privileged people on earth.

We belong to the family of God. And that definitely deserves our most optimistic, "Oh, my!"

❖ ❖ ❖ ❖ ❖

8
Disciples in the Danger Zone

When you walk through the fire,
you shall not be burned . . .

Isaiah 43:2

In our early years of ministry in the Philippines, communist-based New People's Army (NPA) battled the local government to take over the country and convert it to communism. The environment became increasingly hostile and, many times, innocent people got caught in ambushes and crossfire.

On one occasion we conducted a seminar in Bacolod, on the other side of our island, in an open-sided Baptist church situated on the outskirts of town in the middle of a sugar cane field. Pastor Ron Wilkins from Pacific Coast Calvary Chapel in California joined us. Ron had seen a great deal of combat in Vietnam.

And now, as a veteran, he was about to see more.

In the middle of Ron's expository teaching, gunfire exploded around us, rattling our flimsy tin covering. Almost in unison, the 100 pastors in attendance, including Ron and I, hit the floor. The gunfire continued for several minutes, then stopped. Some of the pastors ventured out to a nearby highway, where they found two government soldiers lying dead in the road, ambushed by the NPA. The NPA guerrillas had been hiding in the sugar cane, about fifty yards from the church. One of our pastors discovered his cousin was a casualty. We humbly continued our study, now vividly reminded of the frailty of life.

The southern island of Mindanao became an extreme hot spot for fighting in the Philippines. Although many missionaries left due to threats from the NPA, we continued to do seminars in Mindanao and surrounding islands. One missionary told me he received several threats, the latest a letter with a bullet inside and a note which read: "The next one will be through you!" He left Mindanao for good.

On one trip I flew into the General Santos airport in Mindanao for a seminar and decided to visit a friend, Colonel Farrolin, from Dumaguete City. Debbie and I met he and his wife when we attended Christian Fellowship Church in our home city. He picked me up at the airport.

As we drove the dirt roads surrounded by his convoy of soldiers, Colonel Farrolin explained the NPA often tried to ambush his unit. "They love to get the commanders," he said, which utterly failed to comfort me. "One time," he continued, "we were heading through an isolated area and I felt God telling me to stop the convoy and change jeeps." He obeyed and within fifteen minutes a sniper shot killed the man who'd taken his place in the lead car.

After telling that sunny little story, he asked if I would like to ride in his seat.

I politely declined.

Angels Among the Saints

A Filipino pastor I met at one of our seminars told how he'd been living and pastoring in a mountainous area of the Philippines when the NPA closed in on the area, trying to indoctrinate the locals into communism.

Because of the strong influence of Christianity in the region, the NPA made little impact. So, rebel leaders began to target the Filipino pastor, threatening to murder him if he did not stop preaching the gospel. After much prayer, the pastor and his wife decided they were determined to stay.

One night, a dozen gun toting NPA soldiers showed up at his home, banging doors and demanding he come out. Instead, the pastor and his family got down on their knees and prayed. Soon, rebels became even more heated, ordering the pastor to come out or they would set fire to his home. Unwilling to see his family die, the pastor went outside. The men took him, beat him, and lined him up against a wall for execution.

Many villagers came out of their huts when they heard the commotion, but they could do nothing. The NPA commander turned to the villagers and shouted the pastor must die—and anyone else who refused to follow their orders would die with him. Twelve guns pointed at the pastor, who lifted his hands towards heaven.

"Lord, I am ready to go home. I'm ready to be with You!"

As he stood shivering and his soul ready for the bullets to spray his body, the pastor began to hear something strange.

Click. Click, click. Click. Click, click, click.

Not one gun would fire.

After more clicking and cursing, the commander shouted, "There's a spirit here!"

The men fled as fast as they could run. Fifteen minutes later, villagers heard gunfire in surrounding hills, but the NPA never came back.

The rebel commander spoke the truth; there had been a Spirit there. The Spirit of the Living God! The commander failed to see many angels who stuffed their fingers down the barrels of those guns!

"I know what it means to be kept by Christ Jesus," the pastor smiled.

As we finished studying the book of Jude, he quoted from verse one: "Sanctified by God the Father and preserved in Jesus Christ" (KJV).

What are the odds of twelve guns jamming at one time? Preserved, indeed!

Weathering the Storms

Debbie could rarely travel with me, because of family responsibilities at home. One time, however, I convinced her to come with me to Mindanao, a large southern island. We traveled by boat to Dipolog City, then to the port city of Illigan for our seminar. Upon our arrival we did a portion of the seminar, then checked into the "best hotel in town," an old two-story building, and fell into bed, completely exhausted.

At 4 A.M. our bed began shaking. The floor rumbled and the building swayed. Concrete from the ceiling cracked and pieces fell onto our bed and floor. The power went out. During the earthquake we worked frantically in the pitch blackness to find our clothes and flee the building. As we threw on several pieces of clothes and hurried for the exits, I wondered if the building would collapse.

In the darkness we heard people screaming.

Somehow, the building held.

We stood outside with many other hotel guests, some distraught and crying. Because the hotel stood on top of a hill, about a half-mile from the beach, many people raced to the top, on foot and in cars, to escape the fallout of a potential tidal wave. That night we learned an earthquake hit the area ten years prior, followed by a tidal wave which killed 200 people. Thankfully, on this trip, no tidal wave appeared.

Later in the morning we returned to our hotel and moved out; the earthquake left it in dire need of repair.

Until our work is finished here, we are kept by Him.

Perseverance

Weather often posed a problem in my travels. On one occasion my team and I needed to travel to the next island, Cebu, and then on to another island for our seminar. An approaching typhoon forced the cancellation of our flight. Hurrying to the sea, we tried to catch a one-hour ferry ride to Cebu, but it, too, closed down.

Our only hope was a fisherman who agreed to take us across only after we negotiated to pay him an inflated sum of money. As we made our way across the channel, enormous waves pummeled the boat. By the time we arrived, the storm completely soaked all of us.

Once on the island, we still needed to take a four-hour bus ride up the coast to the big city of Cebu and catch another flight to our island destination. We quickly discovered all of the buses to Cebu were cancelled. We did find a jeep driver who kindly offered to take us . . . for another sizeable fee.

Winds and rain from the fast-approaching typhoon caused havoc, forcing the cancellation of our flight from Cebu to the next island. Once again, we headed down to the sea to look for boat transportation. Fortunately, we found a ship which would take us to the city Cagayan de Oro. Once we arrived, we took an eight-hour bus ride to our seminar destination. Almost comically, we found the bus packed to the brim with passengers, some riding on the roof and others hanging out the windows. Under my seat were three live chickens in a bag and under the seat across the aisle lay a tied-up pig. The overwhelming stench of sweaty bodies and animals filled our nostrils as the rain came down in sheets and the wind howled.

About four hours into the journey, our bus came to a sudden stop. We sat for a long time in traffic, wondering what caused the delay. We soon found out: The storm washed out the bridge ahead.

After standing around for an hour, we were informed of the possibility of crossing the raging river on a man-made bridge. How else could we reach our ultimate destination? On the mission field, you learn to take things as they come!

We decide to try the only way open to us and after a short hike found the bridge. Next to it stood a dark-skinned man with an enormous smile on his face. He collected several pesos from each person who crossed the narrow walking bridge. With all of our bags in tow, we somehow managed to make it across the rickety structure. Once again, we paid a jeep driver handsomely to drive us the remaining four hours to our seminar.

Unfortunately, we arrived two days late.

But what did we find?

One hundred, upbeat pastors, patiently waiting for us.

Together, we enjoyed a rich time in God's Word. The pastors returned to their homes, refreshed and renewed. Once again, God demonstrated His faithfulness as He taught us the importance of perseverance.

Our trip home only took two hours by plane.

❖ ❖ ❖ ❖ ❖

9

Warfare

For we do not wrestle against flesh and blood . . .

Ephesians 6:12

In 1989 I took a trip to Thailand to conduct two Inductive Bible Study seminars. I'll never forget the overpowering presence of evil I felt in that land.

I had come to teach a group of mostly Christian and Missionary Alliance pastors. As I became familiar with my surroundings, I noticed almost every home featured a tiny, doll-like house at the corner of the property. Many Thai people placed food sacrifices in those little houses in an attempt to keep the demons out of their homes.

Buddhist temples filled the land. At one point in our journey, we saw the largest Buddha I had ever seen — at least three stories high, painted bright gold.

All week long I felt a strong oppressive presence. It caused me to pray constantly. After finishing the seminars, I boarded a plane to fly back to Manila. As I sat in my seat, a throbbing headache seemed to crush my skull. I felt totally overwhelmed; I'd never felt such severe pain. It seemed to last forever. Still in immense pain when we landed in Manila, I somehow made it back to my hotel.

Debbie and I planned to meet in Manila to spend some time together before going home. She wanted to purchase some items we couldn't find in our small city. With several hours to go before she was due to arrive, I pulled the blinds and sat in agony.

When Debbie walked into the room, she immediately sensed the presence of evil. Without asking any questions, she began to pray until, finally, I realized the headache completely vanished. It left as quickly as it came.

We were thankful for the deliverance, because we recognized this as an attack of the enemy. Satan saw me vulnerable, without a traveling companion to pray or intercede for me. Since that trip, rarely have I allowed myself to travel alone.

Another attack came as I was preparing to leave for a seminar. I stayed up late to pack and finally retired, only to wake up three hours later, barely able to breathe. I rolled out of bed and began praying but found no relief. I could scarcely take any air into my lungs—I thought I might suffocate. Alarmed, I shook Debbie awake and she got up and began praying.

The attack soon eased, and I could breathe more freely again. I returned to sleep, but when I woke up the next morning, my chest felt tight like the covering of a drum. It hurt to move. I told Debbie I thought I should see a doctor before my flight out in the afternoon. Following a battery of tests, including an EKG, the physician told us he thought I might be having a heart attack. He wanted to put me in the hospital.

When I told him, I couldn't stay because I had a seminar to attend, he got angry and told me I could die if I made the trip. The second he mentioned the word "die," something inside me said, "don't receive it" I've always respected and appreciated the medical profession but, on this occasion, I chose not to take his advice.

After speaking with the doctor for some time, I told him I would go home and get back to him later. Debbie and I tried to pray more at home, but confusion surrounded us. Finally, we decided I should go, do the seminar—and trust Him.

I did go to the seminar and we had an unbelievable week of training. I experienced no trouble breathing and no tightness in my chest. Once back home, I completely forgot about the incident—until about one month later when I received a letter from a lady in my former church. This was before cell phones and instant emails. She was one of our faithful prayer warriors and in her letter, she asked if I was okay.

In the letter, she told me, on a certain day, early one morning as she did her laundry, she started seeing a mental picture of me. She saw someone or something squeezing the air out of my lungs. The image seemed so real it worried and troubled her. Not only did she pray for me, but she called the church prayer line and asked them to pray, too. "I prayed and prayed for you until I felt a peace to stop," she wrote.

Debbie and I got a calendar, examined the date and time the woman saw this vision, and determined it occurred at the exact moment I awakened in the Philippines, gasping for air! Our friend could not possibly have known of my trouble, except by the Spirit of God.

The Power of Prayer—And Praise

Another incident occurred on the home front while I was away conducting a seminar. Debbie awoke at 3 AM in our home, feeling the unquestionable presence of evil at the end of her bed. Although she immediately began to pray against it, the dark presence would not leave. She needed to take the kids to school and felt the presence go with her in the car. She continued to pray as she drove, but to no avail.

After dropping off the kids, she felt impressed to go to the home of one of her prayer partners. Upon arrival, she gave a brief explanation of what was happening and together they determined to sing and worship the Lord. Amazingly, after some time of praise, the evil presence completely left. Worship is a powerful tool to defeat the enemy.

I asked Debbie to tell this next story:

One bright, warm spring morning, our two teenage girls, Lela and Corrie, and I set out to explore the big city of Cebu and do some serious shopping. We'd taken a two-day break from our quiet hometown of Dumaguete and splurged on a short thirty-minute air flight to the nearby island. It was mid-morning as we approached some large department stores. I remembered we'd forgotten to pray, as was our usual morning custom so as we walked, I prayed aloud, quietly asking direction and blessing for the day. I had no idea how significant the prayer would become only two hours later.

Around noon the girls and I decided to get our nails manicured at an affordable price of fifty cents per person. As we enjoyed getting pampered in the small salon, we watched three other ladies get their hair done. Suddenly, three armed men burst in and ordered everyone to lie on the floor. The atmosphere quickly got tense, with nervous gunmen yelling at us for money, watches, and jewelry. The girls and I were lying on the floor, facing each other on our stomachs. One robber pointed his gun a few inches from my head and demanded I give him all my gold earrings, gold necklace, and my wedding ring. He spoke in the local dialect, which I didn't understand, so his demands confused me. He got very angry and intended to rip my earrings out—I have three piercings in each ear, so that is a hunk of ripping. My daughters saw the problem and spoke to him in his language, explaining I would give him what he demanded. I complied, as did all the other ladies in the shop. My heart sank when I saw Corrie hand him the beautiful gold necklace, we had given her for Christmas. I also watched with growing anger as the thieves grabbed Lela's custom-made sapphire ring, we'd recently presented to her as a high school graduation present.

I vividly remember lying on the floor with a gun pointed at my head, praying silently for God's protection. Americans make good targets for radical groups who want to kidnap them for political purposes. I remember the absolute peace which flooded my spirit; I knew whatever happened, God was in control, not the gunmen.

The robbers left the shop a lot wealthier than when they came in, and no one got hurt. Soon the girls and I began talking to the other victims about the holdup. I shared with one lady how little value material things have and how much more value there is in a relationship with Christ. I knew Christians are not exemption from trying circumstances, but we have the absolute assurance God is a very present help in trouble. Once our nerves settled and the police permitted us to leave, I remembered a couple of hundred dollars I had hidden in a side pocket in my purse. We had a decision to make; either cut our shopping trip short and go home, reliving the robbery over and over, or put it behind us and get on with life. "Girls," I said, "I still have money, so let's finish shopping!" And that is just what we did.

One instance from that episode defies human explanation. I had handed my gold wedding band to the robber, who snatched it along with my earrings. I assumed it was gone for good. When the girls and I returned home in the evening, I changed clothes—and to my astonishment, my wedding ring dropped to the floor. I asked the girls if they saw me hand the ring to the robber. "Yes," they said. I have no idea how it got into my clothes, but I told my husband later, "I guess God wants us to stay married!"

As we reflected on their day, Debbie and the girls agreed the afternoon's manicure turned out to be their most expensive ever!

❖ ❖ ❖ ❖ ❖

10

Growing Pains & An Orphanage

*But the Lord is faithful, and He will strengthen
and protect you from the evil one.*

2 Thessalonians 3: 3

As our ministry grew, I realized we needed help. It felt both exciting and scary at the same time, as we brought on new staff who depended on us through a season of extensive travel and rewarding ministry.

One of our board members, Jim Davis, senior pastor at Chapel Mission Viejo, California, visited during our first year in the Philippines. In 1986 he decided the Lord was directing him to join us and moved to Dumaguete with his wife, Shonda, and their four children.

During the first two years, we did four seminars a month. Jim and I traveled more than six months out of the year and time away from our families hurt all of us. Each time we left for two weeks it would take more than a week to re-adjust to the day-to-day family routine. Then we would turn around and take off again. Our marriages and relationships with our children began to suffer.

We decided to stay home for three weeks and venture out for ten days per trip. The new schedule definitely helped our home life, but we still found it extremely difficult to be attentive husbands and fathers.

We hired more staff and sent two teams of teachers spreading out all over the islands. Jim was an invaluable member of the team. He was with us for five years and currently directs Pastoral Training of Asia.

Orphanage in The Makings

Shortly after we adopted Aaron, we realized the dire need for a baby orphanage in our community. The only one in town served low risk babies.
More than 40,000 students attended several colleges in Dumaguete City. Many female students became pregnant and due to their strong Catholic backgrounds and the country's stringent anti-abortion laws, gave birth to their babies and abandoned them at the doorsteps of local hospitals and other places.

When we discovered this great need, Debbie and a Filipino lady, Sophie Montenegro, began praying for God's direction. They prayed faithfully for more than a year and, once again, God answered in a profound way.

On a brief furlough to the States, Debbie and I met Trip Kimball, Senior Pastor of Calvary Chapel Yucca Valley, and his wife, Susan. During our visit, Debbie

had a chance to tell Susan about the orphanage problem in Dumaguete. As Debbie spoke, God was touching Susan's heart. Could God be calling them to help?

At the same time, God began to stir in Trip's heart a desire to train pastors and leaders. Before long they told each other what they were pondering and sought guidance together through prayer.

Two years later, in 1990, Trip resigned from his fruitful pastorate and moved his family to Dumaguete City. Trip began working with Intensive Care Ministries and Susan waited for the vision in her heart to become a reality. I'll let Trip tell the "short version" of how God developed the orphanage: "It didn't take long for the vision to become a reality. Along with help and prayers of Debbie and others with the same vision, Susan began to care for abandoned children. The Social Welfare agency licensed us to be a foster family in March,1991.

Babies kept arriving and by 1993 we needed to change our foster care license to a licensed child caring agency so we could meet the variety of needs presented at our doorstep. We also decided to give the ministry a name, Rainbow Orphanage. The rainbow was God's sign of hope and promise and we believed the home would be a bridge of hope and promise for abandoned children with the goal for them to be adopted.

Soon, our rental home got too small for our growing family.

We prayed and God answered. In December of 1995, a foundation based in the Philippines provided land on which we could build a bigger house for the orphanage. With the help of a work crew from Canada, as well as numerous gifts from churches and individuals, our new home became a reality. The house was almost finished when we moved our three children and all twenty-four babies and children in. We had to carry water inside and didn't have any finished walls or doors, but we felt delighted to have lots of space and a big outdoor play area for the children.

1997 contained both a new door of ministry and a devastating loss. Early in the year a young girl came to us in a state of despair. She was a single student living in a boarding house, twenty-three years old and four months pregnant. She was afraid to go home to her family and didn't want an abortion, but she had nowhere left to turn. We opened our doors to her, and this was the start of the Agape Program, helping unwed mothers and their unborn babies. Agape is the word from the Greek, in the New Testament, for God's unconditional love. The goal for those in this program is that they might find Jesus in a personal relationship and through Him and His unconditional love be healed and set free from past and present hurt and pain.

From 1998 the Agape Program has grown to include educational opportunities and job skill training, as well as residential care for victims of abuse and rape, especially involving incest. Sometimes the girls are as young as eight years old.

Rainbow works with a Social Welfare agency that provides protection, while court cases, sometimes lasting two to three years, are filed against their abusers.

Tragedy struck in August of 1997, only ten days after we moved into our new home. A devastating fire broke out at 4:30 AM. A standing fan in the nursery caught fire and ignited a nearby mattress; within minutes the whole house was ablaze. The fire burned so fast that not all the babies and children made it out alive. Two babies and three young children died that early morning.

Despite the heartbreak and pain of loss, God's love triumphed. Many churches and people locally and abroad gave gifts, money, and labor to rebuild so Rainbow's ministry could continue.

Because Rainbow Orphanage has become more than an orphanage, the name was changed to Rainbow Village Ministries. This village is surrounded by fruit trees, a garden, a piggery, and a big playground for the children. A home for the babies, a home for Agape girls, an office, staff housing, and guest cottages for visitors are all on the compound. The ministry goal has not changed, though. Our goal is to provide hope in a living God, who has a plan and a future for all, from abandoned babies to abused girls. And by His love they will know joy, peace, and experience being part of a Christian family, whether through adoption or those caring for them at Rainbow.

In June of 2014 Rainbow Orphanage closed its facility but the legacy of God's love and compassion lives on in the lives of those who were rescued.

❖ ❖ ❖ ❖ ❖

11

"Home" Calling

*For we walk by faith
and not by sight.*

2 Corinthians 5: 7

Our ministry had become well established as 1990 came to a close. We rented a large, two-story house for the office, where we had our own printing presses, thanks to one of my long-time board members, Pastor John Michaels, and his church, Calvary Chapel Spring Valley of Las Vegas.

Professional printer Lou Correia moved with his family to train our staff to run the presses. We acquired some good computers and a growing staff of loving, competent individuals who knew how to use the equipment. Three teams a month began venturing out to lead Inductive Bible Study seminars. We enjoyed good finances and God blessed the work.

After five years, I began to lose my peace about staying where we were. I prayed for direction. I loved my job and although the training was going extremely well, I sensed the Lord wanting to expand the work beyond the Philippines. Already we had visited Indonesia and Thailand, but I believed the Lord had even broader plans.

Before long Debbie and I agreed we were to leave Dumaguete and head back to the States in order to expand the IBS training into other countries. A more central location would make it easier for me to organize travel plans. We decided on Southern California.

When we announced our move back to the States, our girls felt heart broken. They both cried, not wanting to leave their many friends. They spoke the local dialect, Cebuano, and were totally "plugged in." Lela just completed her first year of college at Silliman University in Dumaguete and Corrie just graduated from high school, while Nathan was entering high school and five-year-old Aaron was getting ready to start kindergarten.

In March 1991, it came time to say goodbye to the many dear friends we'd made and to the country we all called home. The people in our church, where I frequently spoke, held a memorable going away party for us. After many tears and hugs and a long goodbye, we headed back to America. We left the work of training pastors in the capable hands of Pastor Trip Kimball and our gifted Filipino staff.

The return flight took us from Manila to Hawaii, where we stopped for ten days of rest at the invitation of Pastor Mike Stangel of Calvary Chapel North Shore. Mike visited us in the Philippines where he caught the vision for training pastors. His church provided us with a nice home, right on the beach, and gave us a van to drive, a refrigerator full of food, and even some spending money! The whole family felt completely overwhelmed by the congregation's love and generosity.

After a few days, we visited the local grocery store. We told the kids they could each pick out any cereal they wanted for breakfast, but they couldn't wrap their heads around the vast selection of choices. Our choice of breakfast cereal in the Philippines had been very limited. Choices usually consisted of Corn Flakes or no Corn Flakes; it all depended on which missionary family got to the store first.

When we arrived at the checkout counter, Aaron looked mystified by the voice which repeated the price of each scanned item; he searched the checkout area to find the hidden man who read the prices aloud. Then the bag boy spoke up: "Paper or plastic?" We all stood there, baffled. What on earth did he mean? He repeated the question several times before it dawned on us, he was asking what kind of bag we wanted. When we left America six years earlier, plastic grocery bags were not an option.

The surprises and culture shock continued as we became acclimated to our home country once more. On our first trip to the beach, it shocked us to see how tiny ladies' swimsuits were. Where we lived in the PI, women and teen girls often swam in their cloths or at the very least wore a t-shirt over their suits. The kids had other adjustments to make—and quickly. In the Philippines they usually spoke broken English mixed with lots of Cebuano, but who in Southern California would consider that cool?

After Hawaii, we headed for my parents' chicken farm in Mentone, California, where an old, familiar house awaited us. A dozen years earlier we'd moved to Mentone from Texas. Dad owned two acres of land across the street from his home; he invited Debbie and I to build on it. Instead of building, we purchased a freeway move-away house and transported it to the property. It took us months, but we refurbished the home and made it livable. We stayed in the home for a year before moving to Banning to be closer to the church. Since we left Mentone, our old house became a rental and now sat waiting for our return from Asia.

Before leaving the Philippines, I planned to sell our Pinoy. I thought I could make a 100 percent profit, since used cars were in such high demand. We could use the money to buy a decent used car in the States. As I got the vehicle ready to sell, I sensed the Lord nudging: "You need to give away the car, Dan."

"Say what?" I struggled with the concept for several days. I just did not want to give away our car. What would we drive in the States? How would we pay for a new car? It just didn't seem right. Finally, I relented and gave the car to our Philippine ministry.

Back in the States, we had no funds to purchase a car and borrowing family vehicles got old really quick. I received a call from a friend who handled our finances while we lived overseas. He announced his work gave him a brand-new car and he wanted to know, could we use his old car? It ran well and the price was great, free if we wanted it.

God loves it when we quietly obey Him, especially when no one else is watching. How that car blessed us!

Shortly after receiving our gift car, Debbie decided to finish college and get her degree. To do so, we needed another vehicle. Since we couldn't afford one, we made it a matter of prayer. Before long, my sister called asking if we could use a vehicle. She "just happened" to have an extra car and said she would give it to us.

After a year, one of the cars began having major engine problems and we couldn't afford to fix it. My brother, David, took me to a local car dealer and bought me a used Honda Civic, virtually new. As I drove away in our "new" car I rejoiced at how God provided for us. God, you are so good! I reluctantly gave up the old Pinoy and in return You give us three cars. Three! Thank you, Lord.

Through it all, Debbie and I said nothing to anyone about our need for vehicles. We could have dropped hints, but we chose not to. We understood God knew all about our specific needs.

Lessons like these have deepened our knowledge of His faithfulness. Indeed, we've come to realize, the more radical we get in our intensive faith, the more radically faithful He shows Himself.

❖ ❖ ❖ ❖ ❖

12

Football: A Finfrock Passion

Run in such a way that you may win.

1 Corinthians 9: 24

As we settled back into life in California, our oldest son, Nathan, decided he wanted to play football like his dad. In the Philippines he had little exposure to the sport, except for a few televised games my brother videotaped and sent to us.

Nathan was entering ninth grade at Arrowhead Christian Academy in Redlands, California. The school administrator was an old friend, Dr. Darrell Passwater, who just okayed the development of a football program. I first met Darrell in 1969 at Mount Hermon Christian Conference Center while working on summer staff and we have remained friends ever since.

Dr. Passwater was a sports advocate and appointed Jamie Hetricks — a nice young man who loved the game but had no coaching experience — as head coach. When I met Jamie, I said nothing about my own experience, but Jamie eventually found out and asked if I could lend him a hand. I'd already scheduled a few overseas Bible training seminars and knew I would miss several games but thought coaching would allow me to spend some quality time with my son and get more involved in his world.

ACA, still under construction, set up a locker room in the middle of a torn-up building. We had no football field, so we ran the players about a half-mile up the road to a park where we could practice on grass. Jamie and I had fun coaching together. He asked me to put in the offense and defense I used with previous teams. Before I knew it, I found myself calling all the plays and Jamie recommended I take over as head coach which I eventually did. Just before kick-off of our first game, a referee walked up to me and whispered, "Do you realize who you're playing today?"

"Ribét Academy," I replied, "from near downtown Los Angeles."

"That's right," he said. "And they are one of the dirtiest teams I've ever refereed. Your boys better watch their backs."

Our players felt nervous enough, since none of them ever played, so I said nothing about the ref's uplifting comment.

On the opening kickoff a Ribét player came trucking down the field and creamed one of our players. Our boy got up, walked off the field, and said, "Coach, I quit."

The referee frequently flagged the other team and even kicked out several of their players. We hung tough and somehow managed to lose by only two touchdowns. After the game I assured our players, if they kept working hard, eventually we would start winning.

We lost the next week, but I could see improvement. By our third game, we brought home the first-ever ACA football victory. We won four games that inaugural season. At season's end Jamie once more talked to me about taking over as head coach, and I reluctantly agreed.

We won six games in each of the next three seasons, twice made the playoffs and in Nathan's senior year won our first-ever playoff game against Mammoth High School (with snow on the sidelines and temperatures dipping into the teens). Since our expanding overseas ministry required more and more of my time, I planned to turn over the head coaching reins to someone else.

Dr. Passwater convinced me to stay on as head coach one more year. Having a brand- new football field, complete with lights and a beautiful new scoreboard (thanks to one of our biggest fans and supporters, Dr. Alan Kavalich) did influence my decision.

Razzle-Dazzle

During the off-season I found a new offense I thought could really work for us, called the Double-Wing. Few coaches had ever seen it, simply because it tried things no one else dared try. Players lined up foot-to-foot, backs lined up slightly behind ends and the fullback lined up almost right next to the quarterback. It looked like we had no running back in the backfield!

As a play began, one back would swing around, and the play usually moved in the opposite direction. Several of my coaches thought our boys would find it too crazy to use, but the more I showed it to them, the more intrigued they became.

My assistant coach Dave Wiseman and I implemented the Double-Wing in 1995 and went undefeated our first eleven games. The unorthodox offense consistently misdirected the confused defense, with double reverses and all kinds of other unconventional plays. It was hilarious to watch coaches and players as they tried to stop this nightmare offense. Sometimes we sent as many as four players through the hole where the ball carrier would eventually run. Opposing coaches repeatedly called time-outs and barked at their defensive players, all to no avail. We felt almost untouchable — until the quarterfinals of the playoffs, when we finally went down.

I decided to stay another year as head coach. That season we had the best group of high school athletes I'd ever coached. With a solid nucleus of returning players from our 11-1 season, and some remarkable transfer players, we went 14-0 and brought ACA its first-ever CIF Championship in any sport.

Our boys racked up the third highest total of points in California history!

A season like that would keep almost any coach coming back; it did me. Almost our entire team returned in 1997, but we faced a much tougher schedule. After winning our first two games, we faced the defending CIF champs from San Diego, the Bishops. Both squads won sixteen games in a row and they handed us a loss in the final minute of the game.

We finished 11-3 and brought home our second straight CIF Championship, but not before coaching one of the most draining and emotionally intense games of my life. In the semifinals against Lucerne Valley High School, our high-powered offense continually moved the ball down field, but repeatedly turned the ball over at the goal line.

Behind in the last quarter of the game, we marched down the field. With two minutes to go, we pushed the ball within inches of the goal line, but one broken play and another turnover later, we found ourselves on the brink of elimination from the playoffs. We all felt devastated.

Lucerne ran two plays for no gain. Their coach called a timeout and huddled on the field with his players. The next play, Lucerne's quarterback sprinted deep into his own end zone and aired out a long pass. One of our players picked it off and returned it to the 10-yard line. Our team went so crazy we got a 15-yard penalty for over-celebrating.

With less than a minute to play we broke the jinx and jammed the ball into the end zone for the win. The miracle turnaround almost did me in. I think my heart must have stopped five times in the waning moments of that unforgettable game.

I was fortunate to have some outstanding coaches over the years, which I count as one of the greatest keys to our success. We often prayed together before practices and games. Each coach truly cared about the players—and not only about helping them become better athletes, but better young men as well.

Some of my coaches took players aside who struggled in their personal lives, prayed with them and opened up the Bible with them. It felt liberating to be part of a Christian school where there was such freedom. On several occasions we took the boys up to Mammoth Mountains for a few days before our opening game, to get acclimated to the high elevation and spend time together as a team. During our devotions, many players responded to the gospel and invited Jesus Christ into their lives.

For a number of years, I taught first period Bible at ACA. When my players found out about my class, many signed up and enjoyed learning about Inductive Bible Study. I took them through virtually the same class I taught pastors in the Third World, so they learned all the same principles of outlining and charting texts. A few of those young men later went into full-time ministry.

During my classes I told many of my mission stories. The students seemed entranced by the accounts and often asked for more. I wanted them to enjoy Bible rather than just enduring class time. Sometimes when they finished their work, I showed game films. They loved it. They became especially fond of the days when I told them to take out a pen and sheet of paper for a test. Groans were heard. I asked a few simple, no-brainier questions, then walking up to my desk to turn in their papers, I broke out donuts. Instantly I became hero of the day!

A Star Is Born

During all of those years I kept in the back of my mind the idea my youngest son, Aaron, would soon be old enough to play football. He grew up watching our ACA teams, loved the sport, and wanted to play for his dad.

At age six, Aaron ran all over the ballpark. In the middle of one game, as I got ready to call a play, I looked toward the baseball backstop beyond the end zone and saw Aaron perched at the very top. I called a timeout. After scanning the crowd for Debbie, I finally got her attention and pointed to the backstop. Within seconds she sprinted toward our hyperactive son. Aaron spent numerous "time outs" in those early years.

When he began playing Junior All-American Football at age eight, we knew we had a gifted athlete. We videotaped his games, which he would watch for hours. I found time to coach him a little along the way. I soon was going from my daily high school practices to his practices at the local recreation complex.

Aaron became a star player at ACA in his seventh and eighth grade years, under the capable leadership of head coach Willie Guida. Willie ran the kids in practice until they all thought they would drop dead. My players often commented they were glad Coach Willie didn't coach the varsity!
Coach Willie threw in a trick play once in awhile to shake things up, one, I will never forget. He instructed his quarterback yell to the center, "We have the wrong ball. Give it to me." The center picked up the ball and handed it to the quarterback who, in turn, handed it to Aaron, instructing him to take it to the sideline for another ball. While the defense stood in a daze, Aaron sprinted fifty yards down the field for a touchdown.

Coach Willie warned the referees about the play before the game—it was perfectly legal—but the opposing players, coaches, and fans were livid. They became so infuriated I thought we'd have to call the police. Coach Willie took a lot of flak for that episode, but I never heard him retaliate and I never heard of him calling another trick play. His talented team lost only one game in the two years.

Aaron stood only five-foot, four-inches tall and weighed just 135 pounds, but his dedication to weightlifting made him remarkably strong by his senior year. Not only could he bench press more than twice his body weight, but he became the fastest runner ever to play at ACA. What fun we had watching him on a football field, because you never knew when he might break loose for a long touchdown run. In his sophomore season he began as a reserve running back for varsity, but he stepped into a full-time job when a starter got kicked out of school. Aaron ended up having a phenomenal year; he scored two key touchdowns in the championship game when we won our third CIF title.

In Aaron's junior and senior year, he made All League and All CIF, yet we didn't have the team talent as in previous seasons. We went 6-4 both years and lost in the first round of the playoffs. After his last game, we sat in my office for a long time, reflecting on the ACA football program and his career. I let him know how proud I was of him and I would never forget the joy of watching him run like the wind.

Over the years, our whole family got involved in ACA football. Nathan came back the second year after he graduated to help me coach for seven seasons. Debbie became a big fan, sometimes cooking for the team. Our Corrie kept team statistics. During one game I called the same play several times, but it just didn't work. When I started to call it again, Corrie turned to me and said, "Dad, no! You've called the play six times and it hasn't worked yet!" I listened and changed the play.

I retired from coaching in 2003. Never would I have imagined I would coach ACA football for thirteen years, win more than 100 games, take the team to the CIF playoffs twelve times, and play in five CIF Championship games. I didn't come into the job thinking I would build a great football program. At first, I didn't even want to be the head coach.

But when God has a plan, it never gets thwarted. He knew I would love coaching all those impressionable young men, especially my two sons. I realized we didn't enjoy all our success because of my brilliant coaching; because of my busy ministry schedule, I didn't give the program half the time a normal head coach would invest. God simply blessed the works of our hands.

The Big Screen?

Just before Aaron's final high school game in, November 2003, the Los Angeles Times sports editor called to see if they could do a feature story on him. The paper heard how Debbie and I found Aaron near death on a rural road in the Philippines and saw a father son human interest story. The story ran on Thanksgiving Day, with several photographs and details about his life. I considered it one of the best articles ever written about him, and God was honored.

When Aaron and I got our hands on the Times the morning it came out, we both stared for the longest time at the front page of the sports section. We laughed when I noticed Aaron and our family was featured on page one, but Los Angeles Lakers superstar Kobe Bryant was pushed to page three!

About two days after the article came out, we received a phone call from a movie producer in Hollywood. He read the article and wanted to know if we'd be interested in allowing him to do a movie about Aaron's life. His request took Debbie and I by surprise. We told him we would need to think about it and get back to him. In the meantime, we did some research and discovered this producer had done several good films. We decided to talk with him further.

A week later he and his wife spent a few hours with us at our home. He assured us he would try to keep the film as true to Aaron's real-life story as possible. We would have final approval.

As the producer's writers went to work on the film script, Aaron was on cloud nine and even asked if he could do some of his own parts. About two weeks later the producer called and told us while his writers had come up with two solid acts, he needed a third to make it a good movie. He thought the project reached a dead-end for the time being, but perhaps down the road Aaron's life would lend itself to the all-important third act.

None of us had any idea how dramatic the final scene would turn out to be!

❖ ❖ ❖ ❖ ❖

13

An Unforgettable Meeting

I will bring the blind by a way they did not know,
I will lead them in paths they have not known . . .

Isaiah 42:16

After our move back to the States in 1991, I remained in limbo for six months. I knew I was to develop our Inductive Bible Study ministry in different countries, but I did not know where to go next. I've always found it difficult to wait on the Lord's direction and timing, simply because His ways often differ so much from the way I envision things should unfold.

One day I got a call. Pastor Chuck Smith from Calvary Chapel Costa Mesa wanted to know if I could attend a meeting regarding Russia. Dr. Bill Bright of Campus Crusade for Christ along with some of his staff would be sharing with several Calvary Chapel pastors. I headed to Costa Mesa for the meeting, feeling awed by those in attendance. It seemed humorous to see Dr. Bright, Paul Eshelman, and the Crusade staff, wearing suits and ties, while Pastor Chuck, Greg Laurie, Raul Ries, Mike MacIntosh, Don McClure, Brian Brodersen, and other Calvary Chapel pastors were wearing T-shirts and Levis.

Dr. Bright described how Crusade had been showing the popular Jesus film all over Russia; estimates said close to a million viewed the movie and thousands surrendered their lives to Christ. Some of the top leaders in Russia saw the film and become believers!

With all these converts, Dr. Bright expressed a tremendous need for churches to disciple the new believers. Most of the mainline denominations in Russia, showed little interest in reaching out. Campus Crusade desperately needed churches to help with disciplining all these new believers. Dr. Bright approached Pastor Chuck for help, because he knew Calvary Chapel did not have a lot of red tape to work through before it could act, as did many denominations.

I found the meeting fascinating. My heart was stirred when I heard what God was doing in Russia. Dr Bright concluded by asking Pastor Chuck if Calvary Chapel could help. It seemed like an eternity passed as Pastor Chuck sat there, saying nothing. Then he turned and looked intently at me — to the point where I became increasingly uncomfortable.

Finally, Pastor Chuck asked me to describe our work in the Philippines. I felt dumbfounded to suddenly get thrust into the spotlight before all of these men. I felt totally unprepared to speak on anything.

I stuttered badly as I started off, but I began to relax and explained how we'd seen a great deal of success in training Filipino pastors to study the Word of God more effectively. When I related everything, I could think to say, Dr. Bright looked me in the eye and said, "That is exactly what we need in Russia!"

Pastor Chuck peered at me with a knowing grin and said, "Well, Dan, when can you go?"

To Russia, With Love

Two months later I found myself flying to Moscow.

Just before I purchased my tickets, I contacted Dr. Bright to see if he could get me in touch with some contacts in Moscow. He didn't hesitate to say the time I'd chosen for my visit was not ideal; many Crusade staff would be gone for Christmas. He suggested I visit at a different time.

After praying, I still thought I should go in December. I called Dr. Bright to tell him, and he responded very graciously. He asked me to come to Campus Crusade headquarters at Arrowhead Spring, near the base of the San Bernardino Mountains in California. I drove over and met with him for close to three hours. He treated me warmly, like an old friend. Before I left, he prayed over me. I left extremely encouraged.

Shortly before I left for Russia, I spoke at a church, when service ended a printer named George Sparks approached me. George had a special interest in Russia and asked if he could join me. I was happy to have his company.

George and I headed to Moscow without any plans set in stone. Instead, we wanted to meet whomever the Lord brought across our path and do whatever He asked us to do. We had no clue what lay ahead.

About half-way to Moscow I read a powerful Scripture: "I will bring the blind by a way they do not know I will lead them in paths they have not known. I will make darkness light before them, and crooked places straight. These things I will do for them, and not forsake them" (Isaiah 42:16). I knew this verse spoke of the children of Israel and God's promise to help them, but I also knew God meant it for George and me on our journey.

We arrived at the ancient, rundown Sheremetyevo International Airport in Moscow and made our way through customs. The dark, dingy walls and ceiling seemed to match the old, dilapidated cars outside. We took a taxi to our hotel. The temperature dropped into the teens and I was extremely thankful for the hooded parka jacket I'd borrowed. The dull, gray buildings around Moscow seemed to mirror the lack of color everywhere.

Our room was on the thirty-fifth floor in one of three large hotels built specifically for the Olympic Games in the '60s. As George and I walked down a long hall of rooms, just two rooms from ours, a door stood open and we heard people speaking English. I stuck my head in and introduced myself; to our amazement, they worked with Campus Crusade. A delay in their travel plans forced them to wait, but before they departed, they introduced us to a young Russian believer named Alex, who would serve as our guide.

Our first full day in Moscow Alex took us by subway to a local church meeting in a theater. We found the church packed with hundreds of people on Sunday; the atmosphere felt exhilarating and electric. Many went forward during the altar call. God was at work! After the service, Alex introduced us to an assistant pastor, an American, who told how a door was miraculously opened for them to start the church only a year before. Almost overnight it grew into a Spirit-filled house of worship, complete with its own Bible school. When the church leaders heard about our Inductive Bible Study, they invited us to return and teach the course.

Someone asked if we had any contacts with the underground churches; when we replied "no," they arranged for us to meet with a leader. Soon we found ourselves on a train headed for St. Petersburg.

They instructed us to sit tight once we pulled into the city, someone would contact us. Sure enough, a Russian man and his translator hopped onto the train and introduced themselves. The Russian had a job as a physician, which served as a "front" for his role as a leader of the underground church. He was excited to hear of our ministry and arranged for us to return in March to teach their pastors our IBS seminar.

Again, and again, God sovereignly connected us with key people in Moscow and other cities. We flew back to America more excited than ever about what God wanted to do with IBS training.

March 1992, I traveled back to Russia and led our first-ever IBS training there, with fifty students at a church Bible school in Moscow. Next, I took the overnight train to St Petersburg to conduct our second seminar.

Our Russian friends got me a room in a five-star hotel for just five dollars a day. The conference took place in a beautiful auditorium with bright red carpeting. More than 150 underground pastors and leaders came from many cities.

I taught those pastors as I stood behind a podium displaying a picture of the hammer and sickle. A chill ran down my spine as I began to realize the incredible opportunity the Lord had given me. This very hall hosted communist party meetings, but I'd been sent to teach pastors from various cities in Russia, God's Word.

Several pastors did not want to do the assignments we gave them. They believed in divine revelation and reasoned they didn't need to study. "How do you teach the Bible?" I asked.

"We come before our congregations on Sunday and wait," one replied. "We wait until God moves us into a certain text."

After dialoging with them for some time, we opened the Bible together. "Be diligent to present yourself approved to God, a worker who does not need to be ashamed, rightly dividing the word of truth," I quoted from 2 Timothy 2:15. When Paul says to be diligent, he is clearly instructing Timothy to study the Word. The more we study, the more divine revelation we will receive!

For the first time, these pastors began to examine the Scriptures in context. Boy, did they get excited when they sensed God speaking to them, directly from His Word!

Day two of the seminar in St. Petersburg brought something of a shocker. The Russian media showed up, toting notepads and TV cameras. They interviewed me during a break, and I described the seminar and even gave a short gospel message. That night I watched myself on the news and wondered what kind of repercussion the story would generate.

When we arrived at the seminar the next day we heard right after the news broadcast, a memo had been sent to the entire Russian Orthodox priesthood warning priests against attending our seminar. Once we started, it amazed us to see a number of brave Russian Orthodox priests in attendance, obviously eager to learn more.

Desperate Passage

As the months passed, more requests flooded in for seminars. I decided to return in July, but I ran into all kinds of snags trying to set up the details from the States. The leaders who invited me simply didn't understand all of the planning, complexities, and details which went into organizing a successful seminar.

In desperation I called my number one assistant in the Philippines, Bobby Café, and asked if he could travel to Russia paving the way for my visits. Bobby, a former bank manager, became an expert at going ahead of our teams to iron out the details.

"Pastor Dan," Bobby said, pausing a long time before continuing. "I've never been to Russia and I don't speak their language."

"Don't worry," I assured him. "We'll provide a translator; it will be just like in the Philippines."

Bobby agreed to go, but none of us had any idea what he'd have to overcome.

To make sure things went smoothly, I paid a translator to purchase Bobby's train tickets and to travel with him. Things started out well enough. The translator picked up Bobby at the airport, took him to the train station, and got him on the train. But then said, "I'm sorry, this is as far as I go. Something's come up and I can't travel with you." Bobby protested, but the translator made it clear he would not accompany him anywhere. He gave Bobby only one bit of advice: "After eight hours on the train, about 25 stops, you get off." And then he disappeared.

As the train rumbled down the tracks, Bobby searched vainly for someone who spoke English but to no avail. Although he traveled in a sleeper car, Bobby was afraid to go to sleep. Nerves frazzled after close to eight hours of travel, Bobby lost all count of the number of stops the train made. He fervently prayed God would show him where to get off.

At one of the next stops, something nudged Bobby and he knew the time had come for him to exit. He grabbed his luggage and jumped off the train before he could change his mind. Going with the flow of people exiting the train depot, he boarded a bus and, for the next four hours, road around the city six times. Finally, he spotted a hotel with some English words on its sign, so he hopped off to find someone who spoke English.

No one did. Bobby tracked down a receptionist who did understand Bobby's sign language. He convinced her to telephone the pastor with whom Bobby would ultimately meet. After getting no answer for hours, the receptionist finally reached the pastor and told him a Filipino man who didn't speak Russian wanted to meet him.

Within minutes, the pastor arrived to rescue Bobby. After spending several hours together, they got the details worked out for the upcoming seminar—mission accomplished. The pastor put Bobby on a train for Moscow, where he would catch another train to the next seminar location. Once again, Bobby had no one to guide him or translate for him. During the passage to Moscow, he fretted because he knew when he reached Moscow, he would have to purchase another ticket to his second destination.

Standing in line at the train depot and not knowing how he was going to tell the ticket seller the name of his destination city, Bobby prayed earnestly—and heard a voice from behind, speaking in perfect English.

"Where are you going?"

Bobby turned around, practically hugging the English-speaking stranger.

Not only did the stranger help Bobby purchase his ticket, but he gave him explicit instructions when to get off the train and where to go from there. Bobby insists the man was an angel sent to help him.

And perhaps he was, because Bobby made it to his next location without a hitch. He set up the second seminar and managed to look only a bit shaken.

Suitcase Sidebar

After Bobby had paved the way, our team landed in St. Petersburg and made it to baggage claim with no problems. Soon we discovered the luggage of one of our team members, Dr. Bill Cullins, failed to show up. Dr. Cullins had a successful chiropractic practice in Hemet, California; he has treated both Debbie and I for years. He always dresses sharply in good looking clothes. Bill lost both suitcases on the flight and never saw them again.

For the next two weeks, poor Dr. Bill wore the same shirt and pair of Levi's he'd traveled in. We scoured local stores but could find very little clothing; and what we did find wouldn't fit Dr. Bill's large frame.

Dr. Bill washed his lone shirt and pair of Levis each night, hanging them out to dry. Many a morning he found them still damp. But he wore them anyway.

Even though I could tell he struggled with his clothing situation, he seldom complained. In fact, even wearing those damp clothes, Dr. Bill treated many seminar attendees who suffered from aching backs, necks, and bodies. The people went home at night and told all their friends about the doctor with the damp clothes who knew how to heal their aches and pains.

Dr. Bill became the most popular man around. Every day, growing numbers of people lined up for treatments from this doctor who not only adjusted them but prayed for them. No one cared Dr. Bill wore the same clothes every day, because many did the same.

Although Dr. Bill survived the trip and made a remarkable impact, I felt sure he would never want to return. To my surprise, he told me God spoke to him about his excessive wardrobe which he was determined to get under control.

Dr. Bill accompanied me on many more trips to Russia over the next few years, as well as to several other countries. I felt about him much as the apostle Paul must have felt about Dr. Luke—a faithful traveling partner for whom I'll always be grateful.

❖ ❖ ❖ ❖ ❖

14

An Unsuspecting Leader

And my message and my preaching were not in persuasive words of wisdom,
but in demonstration of the Spirit and of power, so that your faith
would not rest on wisdom of men, but on the power of God.

1 Corinthians 2:4

During our second trip to Russia, the same translator who backed out of our deal to serve as a guide for Bobby Café also missed our seminar which he committed to translate. We had 100 pastors and church leaders gathered to learn Inductive Bible Study, but no one to translate.

As pastors came from miles around, it appeared as if we might have to cancel. I felt heartbroken and furious, because all the materials were ready to go. The learners had come, so we prayed like crazy.

Our host, who could speak some English but could not translate, got up in front of the participants and asked if anyone could translate. One young man in the crowd spoke fluid English and even taught English in school but said he could not do it.

Igor Prokopiev, a brand-new Christian who knew no Christian terminology, had come with a small group of young people. A mainline denominational church recently kicked him out, along with his new wife, Olga, and their group, because as they prayed for revival, some of them suddenly began speaking in tongues. They had no idea what happened, so they went to their pastor to inquire about it. He removed the whole group from the church because he thought speaking in tongues was of the devil.

This group heard about our seminar and came eager to learn how to get into the Word. When we told the participants, we'd have to cancel the seminar because of no translator, these friends closed in around Igor, laid hands on him, and prayed passionately over him.

Reluctantly, Igor agreed to translate, and we began the seminar. During each break, as we worked through the day, Igor's group gathered around him to pray for him. He did extremely well and at times got so excited about the Bible studies he would literally jump up and down.

"This is so good! This is so good!" he would declare.

One evening I sat up late, talking with Igor and listening to his testimony. At one time he'd been a very popular rock singer, abusing drugs and wild living. One night while sleeping with a thirteen-year-old prostitute, he awoke out of a dead sleep to a voice saying, "Igor, what are you doing with your life?"

He laid there wide awake, heart pounding. Soon the guilt of his sinful life overwhelmed him like a tidal wave. He fell out of bed to his knees, pleaded for forgiveness, and begged Christ to come into his life. Shortly after, he met Olga his future wife and led her to Christ.

Toward the end of the seminar I asked Igor if he would like to become Intensive Care Ministry's first full-time Russian staff member. Igor's face became puzzled. He told us God seemed to speak to him some time back about stepping out into ministry full time. Igor did not understand what it meant at the time, but that night he accepted our invitation. Igor served with us for 26 years and currently is involved in other ministry opportunities.

As our seminars progressed, we enjoyed watching the excited reactions of the participants. Prior to the seminar, a few pastors and Christian workers commented, "How are you going to keep the attention of the participants such a long time?" After the first day, they looked on, dumfounded and exhilarated by the new discoveries everyone was making in God's Word.

God amazed us, too, at how He allowed the excitement about the study to spread to so many people in so many completely unplanned ways. We couldn't have orchestrated the reaction if we tried.

For example, while doing a seminar in the once-closed military city of Nikolayev, Ukraine, the doors of the room suddenly burst open and the local television media poured in. At first it upset me because the reporters made so much noise and the bright camera lights distracted students from the lesson. As the camera rolled, however, I decided to share the gospel.

In the evening, the only news station in Nikolayev—a metropolis of more than 500,000 people—carried the story of Intensive Care Ministries. And they broadcast my short gospel message! Who knows how God used His Word to transform lives? His Word never returns void.

❖ ❖ ❖ ❖ ❖

15
Why, God?

For My thoughts are not your thoughts,
nor are your ways My ways...

Isaiah 55:8

So often we have our own pre-planned notions about the way things should go. We think because we're "serving God," everything should work out precisely as we planned. We have a vision for God's will. We think we're doing what He wants....

Then the unexpected happens.

We cry, "Why God? I don't understand!"

In the summer of 1996, we returned to Russia for more Inductive Bible Study training. When Igor and I traveled to Cherpovets, the KGB informed me that my visa had was drawn up incorrectly and I had twenty-four hours to get out of town. I returned to Moscow to get the problem worked out. Igor went ahead to teach the seminar without me and did a great job.

By the time my visa got corrected, the seminar in the north almost ended, so I returned to Cherpovets and focused on training church leaders. On my second day, one of my legs—on which I'd had surgery several years earlier to repair a torn Achilles—started causing me severe pain. It got so bad I was forced to stay in bed for several days.

I became depressed and discouraged. Why did God allowed me to make the trip? Nothing had gone according to plan. I continued to pray and did some deep soul-searching about my life and the direction of ICM.

As the leg began to improve, Igor's church, Christ's Church of Cherpovets, asked me to speak on our last night in the city. Five years earlier I encouraged a small group of young people to start the fellowship, which now numbers more than 600.

After some powerful worship, the pastor asked the congregation to give a special offering to our organization. He explained to his congregation that it was important to plant some "seeds" towards ICM. As the offering plates circulated, the voices around me rang out in Russian the words to a favorite song: "He who began a good work in you will be faithful to complete it."

In an instant the Lord affirmed to my heart, His desire to complete the good work He had started through ICM some twelve years earlier. He reminded me while my vision can grow foggy, His remains crystal clear. My focus is temporal, but His is eternal. My resources are limited, but His are limitless.

My depression completely left. My Spirit felt light and free, as if God lifted 500 pounds from my back. The special offering came to more than $300, a phenomenal amount of money for this poor church. They gave out of their poverty and God's encouragement overwhelmed me.

An Unexpected Cancellation

Another time we also felt tempted to question, "Why, God?" Igor, Olga, and I scheduled back-to-back seminars in Russia. We invested a great deal of time and money in each when organizers of the seminar abruptly announced they needed to cancel.

We had a good relationship with this group, so it shocked us they would cancel, especially within days of the event. We spent a lot of money to reserve a conference center and hotel rooms. I sent Igor ahead of us to see if we could do anything to reconcile the situation.

When Igor arrived, he learned this conservative group heard from their home denomination our ministry had a connection to Calvary Chapel of Costa Mesa, which they considered a cult. The denomination immediately ordered their Russian director to cancel our seminar. When I heard the allegations, I could only shake my head in disbelief.

We couldn't get a refund at that late date, so Igor started canvassing the city, inviting everyone and anyone to come to our seminar. When we arrived, thirteen people showed up, including ten women and no pastors.
It totally bummed me out.

"Why, Lord? Why did You allow this to happen?"

We went ahead and did the seminar. I felt completely frustrated and discouraged, mainly because we'd spent considerable resources and yet hadn't reached a single pastor.

"Why would God do such a thing?" I grumbled. "It doesn't make any sense!"

Proverbs 3:5 says "... lean not on our own understanding but acknowledge Him in all our ways ..." but my flesh reacted, and I remained ticked off. Mid-morning the second day, a woman in the seminar began weeping loudly. I told our group to take a break and approached her. With the help of our translator I discovered she was not a believer and the Holy Spirit was exposing her sin.

101

I shared the gospel and asked if she would like to invite Christ into her life. She wanted to but said she could not because she was "a terrible sinner."

I told her we were all sinners, saved only by the grace of a loving Savior. She wept even louder, almost convulsing, saying I did not understand her awful sinfulness. Again, I assured her Christ came to save the vilest of sinners.

"God cannot forgive me!" she blurted out. "I am living with a man—a married man!"

I continued to explain Christ's unconditional love, He had His hands and feet pierced to set her free of all her sin and guilt. She agreed to pray with me. and as we did, I could sense the weight of her sins lifting off her. When we finished praying, her face virtually glowed.

Nevertheless, I still felt bummed out about the seminar, grumbling because we reached no pastors.

Until the next day.

Another woman in the seminar burst out in tears, obviously struggling with something. Again, I stopped the seminar to speak with her. After a short time, she surrendered her life to Christ. As we prayed, I'll never forget how God rebuked me, "I am God, and I will do what I desire to do, even if it does not seem cost effective to you!"

One year later when we did more seminars in the same area, one of these two ladies approached me during a break and gave me an enormous hug. With great exuberance she said, since we last saw each other, she led her mother and brother to Christ, along with ten of her friends.

God indeed works in mysterious ways! When will I learn to go with the flow? When will I decide simply to love Him, desire to please Him, and let the chips fall where they may?

Tracts and Bibles Galore

During one excursion from Poland to Moscow, we got delayed at the border of Russia when workers gathered around our train, put it on a hydraulic lift, and began to change the wheels so they could fit the wider tracks in Russia.

While our train sat precariously in the air, one of our team members began a conversation with a passenger heading in the opposite direction on a train directly across from ours. (It needed to undergo the reverse procedure to fit the narrower tracks in Poland.) One thing led to another and our team member began witnessing about Christ. Soon, the windows all around that passenger began going down. Other passengers wanted to hear the conversation.

When our team member asked the passenger if he would like a Christian tract, the man said yes. He looked as if he were about to receive a wonderful gift. But we had a problem.

There was no way to get the tract to him.

One of our team asked a worker below if he would pass the tract over to the man in the train. As the worker obliged, other passengers began asking for tracts as well. Our greasy-handed worker found himself passing out tracts like free food!

Someone from our team broke out some extra Bibles, which we passed out to our new worker friend, his coworkers, and other people on our train. The work on both trains quickly came to a virtual standstill as these workers huddled together, reading their tracts and Bibles.

After several minutes an enormous Russian—clearly the boss—approached to find out what was causing the delay. He yelled at his

103

people to get back to work, but no one listened to him. He spoke to his workers, then came directly toward us. We thought for sure we were in big trouble.

He peered up at us. "I want a Bible, too!"

Were we ever happy to give him one!

When we finally pulled away from the border, we saw the workers, gathered in little groups, reading their tracts and Bibles.

In those early days of freedom from communism, you could get mobbed simply by handing out tracts and Bibles. The people had an incredible hunger for the truth, unfortunately, things have changed. The limited window of time to fill a gaping spiritual void is slowly closing. The Western world has invaded Russia with materialism, pornography, and cults, polluting the truth. Unfortunately, the Russian government is again limiting Christian freedom.

❖ ❖ ❖ ❖ ❖

16

Sudan And Back? Or Not . . .

And my God shall supply all your need
according to His riches in glory by Christ Jesus.

Philippians 4:19

In the summer of 1997, I was asked to teach the Inductive Bible Study class to a group of pastors in Sudan, Africa. I would be part of a team of doctors, nurses and several Calvary Chapel Pastors. At first, I thought it sounded like a great idea, but I began to learn more about the trip from Pastor Ed Cornwell, who was filling me in on the bleak current events in that war-torn country. As I heard of the atrocities, I began having doubts about making the trip.

Sudan had plunged into a bloody civil war. Northern Sudan, governed by Muslims, battled Southern Sudan, a predominantly Christian region. Southern Sudan had been fighting for its freedom for twenty years, resulting in more than two million deaths.

This country brimming with strife and persecution saw its roads and railroads destroyed. Supplies ran short and many people starved to death. The Sudanese people grew crops to feed themselves, only to have them burned or stolen by Muslim government raiders on horseback. Raiders attacked villages and burned their homes, killing everyone in sight. They even kidnapped healthy children and sold them into slavery. These were brutal times for the people of Southern Sudan.

Once I agreed to make the trip, Debbie and I received release papers from the organization which would take us into the country. They wanted Debbie to sign a statement agreeing she would not sue their organization if I got killed. And once more, the realization I could lose my life began to concern us.

After we sought the Lord, we both knew I was supposed to join the team.

On the day of departure, I spoke at Calvary Chapel Pacific Coast in their two morning services. Before I began teaching from the Word, I briefly described my upcoming trip so people could pray for me. After each service, men and women came up to encourage me; many of them handed me money. In all my years of speaking in other churches, this rarely happened. I stuck the money in my pocket and forgot about it. As Debbie drove me to LAX, I remembered the money and pulled it out. I found several $100-dollar bills, along with a bunch of other denominations (no pun intended). I don't need this money, I thought. Maybe I should just leave it with Debbie. But something inside said, "Take it with you." so I hung onto the bills.

Two days later I arrived in Nairobi, Kenya, and discovered the plane our team booked to take us into the Sudan needed repairs. We paid a large sum of money to reserve the plane, but the company said no other equipment was available; we would have to wait. We waited three days, but still no plane, we tried to get a refund and find another company to fly our team to Sudan.

We finally found a crew who would fly us, but it could not accommodate our whole team (two doctors, two nurses, six pastors, and a ton of rice and medical supplies). We needed to reduce our team and take fewer supplies. One doctor and two pastors volunteered not to go.

Our advance team of Wes Bently and a Sudanese pastor had flown in ahead of us to make sure of the area's safety, but we hadn't heard from them in more than six days. We couldn't wait any longer. We needed to decide whether to go in, safe or not. We chose to go.

The trip began with a two-hour flight to a border airport where we refueled. As we waited, Ed warned us not to talk with anyone hanging around our plane. He said sometimes the Northern Sudanese government had spies at the airport through whom information would be given to the government.

One ministry group had come to the same airport and freely talked about their mission. After they landed on a dirt airstrip in Southern Sudan and began to unload their supplies, government gunship helicopters buzzed in, shot up all their supplies, and killed several people.

We continued on our flight for the next four hours until we spotted a tiny dirt landing strip below. Our large African pilot pointed to a wall of black clouds looming in the distance and said he did not want to land the plane.

"If it rains, the runway will turn to mud," he said. "There will be no way out."

After arguing with him for several minutes, he banked sharply, agreed to give it just one try. He skillfully brought the plane in for the quickest landing I'd ever experienced. Before we came to a stop, he yelled at the top of his lungs, "Get off this airplane. Get off this airplane, now!"

We grabbed as many of our things as we could and jumped onto the airstrip. The pilot heaved the remains of our luggage and supplies onto the runway. Just before he turned the plane to leave, we told him we would see him in five days. I will never forget his response. He glanced at us with those large, brown eyes and said, "Maybe." The plane jerked, turned, and rattled and rumbled down the runway, lifting into the air just as the rain started coming down in torrents.

Our team had no time to put on our ponchos and we got soaked. Wes and his guide, along with a large number of excited Sudanese people, greeted us. Their satellite phones malfunctioned, becoming useless, so they couldn't contact us.

I heard gunfire in the distance.

As we set up our tents around a building half destroyed by bombs, we noticed many other homes and buildings burned to the ground. We learned rebel soldiers recently overran the area.

Rags fell from the emaciated bodies of the people and hunger seemed to seep from their hollow eyes. We quickly set up a crude clinic and hundreds of people lined up to see the doctor. They streamed through for hours; some could barely walk. Our doctor tried to take the worst cases first, but quickly found himself overwhelmed by the sheer number of urgent needs. As night fell, we had to stop and send people away.

Our travel problems delayed our arrival by three days. We found out some pastors came and waited for two days, then left; some went home the very day we arrived. We sent a message to many, but most responded it would be too dangerous to attempt a return. My heart sank as I realized I could not minister to those willing pastors.

For the next five days I assisted the medical team by sorting medications and purifying fresh water with my hand pump. The town well was broken, sending people to the filthy river, which carried numerous diseases. One disease caused blindness if untreated; unfortunately, we saw multiple cases of this river blindness. The drug needed to cure the ugly disease cost very little, but without drug stores and doctors, these poor people had little hope.

Area leaders told us kidnappers recently took twelve local children in a raid and would soon sell them into slavery. The leaders knew the location of the children but insisted they could do nothing to save them.

Ed asked if it would be possible to purchase the children back.

It would require several hundred dollars, but a deal might be possible. Ed described the need to our team, and we all emptied our pockets. Thanks to the generosity of the brothers and sisters at Calvary Chapel Pacific Coast, and to the kindness of our other team members, we came up with enough money for the trade. We heard later the children's freedom had been purchased and they were returned safely to their homes.

Added Blessing

An interesting sidebar to this story occurred in the US about a month after our trip. During a seminar in Kentucky I told the story of the twelve kidnapped children. When the seminar concluded, one participant came up to me and shared this story:

"I was at Calvary Chapel Pacific Coast the Sunday you spoke!" he said. "God directed me to give you some money for your trip, but when I looked in my wallet, All I had was a $100 bill. To be honest, I didn't want to give that much. I struggled and struggled, but finally I decided to give it."

I told him he played a big part in bringing those children home. He felt overwhelmed and thankful he'd obeyed.

Losing My Appetite

On the third day of our Sudan trip, I walked up a trail with one of our guides, en route to a church about a mile away from our "headquarters". I wanted to meet the pastor and see the grounds. As we walked, a young girl joined us. She reported how her father died a year earlier in a raid. The girl's mother struggled to feed the girl and her three siblings.

"My mother said she wanted to move to the North to get out of all the fighting, but if we did, we would be forced to convert to Islam," the girl said. "My older brother stood up to my mother! He told her if our father died in Southern Sudan as a Christian, we should also stay and die as Christians!"

When we arrived at the church, I noticed a hole in the roof about the size of a surfboard. We learned a bomb dropped through the ceiling, smashed to the ground directly in front of the podium, and yet never exploded. The hole in the roof provided the perfect amount of light for the speaker's podium!

The leader of the church, a young man in his early twenties, had taken over after the pastor fled for his life. The young man did not know how to teach from the Bible, so instead, he simply read it. Not a bad concept! I talked to him about how to break a text apart and prepare a Bible study. He accepted an Inductive Bible Study manual and expressed gratitude for the new tools he now possessed to understand the Scriptures.

We heard of a school next to the church but learned all the classrooms remained empty. "There are no teachers," the people told us. "The teachers are trying to survive. They are out farming for food to live on." Few had time to educate children in starving Southern Sudan.

I saw many mothers who outwardly favored one or two of their children. Often, due to lack of food, they were forced to choose which children they would feed and which they would allow to starve to death. Barely clothed children with bloated stomachs wandered about everywhere, surrounded by flies. Some people were so weak they lacked the strength to bury their own dead. The stench of death permeated the land. Lines to see our doctor grew longer each day. The people just sat there in the hot sun all day, hoping for help.

At the beginning of our stay we took lunch breaks. Many eyes watched us, because we couldn't hide to eat. We gave away much of our food, but most of it proved too rich for the people; it made them sick. It was completely overwhelming to see such deep needs and yet feel so ineffective in doing anything about it. I watched as different team members became depressed and simply dropped to the ground burying their heads in their hands quietly crying. After our second day of seeing so many starving and sick people, I couldn't even eat.

The Sudanese people's dire circumstances made my stomachache, but so did the danger of our location. My neck and shoulders often tensed as gunfire erupted in the distance, a constant reminder of the intense, nearby fighting.

At times I wondered if we would ever get out of this country alive. I thought of Debbie and the children and wondered how they would live if I failed to return. I thought about my football team and what a wonderful bunch of kids were coming back in the fall. What a bummer to miss out on coaching them to their second CIF Championship!

The pilot's last words about coming back for us echoed in my mind: "Maybe," he warned. Maybe he wouldn't return. Fear threatened to choke me and suffocate my spirit. The words of the Bible became medicine for my soul. It brought peace to my heart as I meditated on its abiding truth. I must trust Him. My life was in His hands.

The Treasure of Clothes

Clothes become a valuable commodity in Southern Sudan because of their scarcity. Almost every day at least one resident would ask to trade a spear or knife for our clothing. By the end of the week, I traded or gave away all of my clothes, including my treasured CIF Championship T-shirt. In the process, I collected several nice spears which I planned to take home to give to my family and friends.

On the last day of our journey a tall, thin Sudanese man approached the doctor on our team and asked if he would trade his pants for a spear.

The doctor, who stood five feet and weighed over 200 pounds, possessed one extra pair of pants and agreed to make the trade.

Several minutes after making the deal, the Sudanese man came walking toward us wearing his new, baggy pants and smiling ear-to-ear. I will never forget his smile — or those big pants.

How could we call giving away our clothes a "sacrifice" at all? We will go home and replace everything we left behind. But these poor people could only wait and hope for the next foreigners to come in — and if they were lucky, trade for some clothes.

Any clothes.

The Plane Truth

On our last day we headed down the trail toward the dirt airstrip. We all wondered if our plane would show up. I felt anxious to go. We had experienced an emotionally draining and life-changing trip and someday I wanted to return. But at that moment, I wanted to take to the skies.

We prayed all week the rain would stay away, and God answered our prayers. As we stood in the open field of the dirt runway, we heard the noise of a plane. My heart soared!

But something seemed wrong.

The Sudanese began screaming and everyone scattered, taking cover in the nearby brush. The plane overhead, we learned, was a government fighter jet. If the pilot saw us, he would blast everything in sight. Fortunately, he did not spot us. We stayed under cover until we heard another plane buzzing in the distance.

Ours!

Watching our little plane bank toward us was one of the most welcome sights ever. The pilot brought her in, rolled her down the bumpy runway, drew her to a stop, and immediately began refueling. We quickly loaded our things before anything else could go wrong.

Many of our precious Sudanese friends hurried out to send us off. As they waved goodbye it hurt to face the reality most of them probably wouldn't live long. Most Americans can't fathom the devastation and hardships these precious people face. I felt I'd just spent a week in hell.

Back Home

I have a picture etched in my mind of our team shuffling out of customs in Los Angeles, arms full of large bundles containing menacing spears and homemade Sudanese knives. We looked like a victorious guerilla army returning home with all kinds of booty. We got lots of stares, but had no trouble marching right through customs.

How times have changed!

I felt blessed to return to America, the land of plenty. I thanked God He chose to place us here, to raise our family and establish a ministry base in this wonderful free land. Every time I come home from an overseas trip, I appreciate the United States of America more and more.

For many months I could not get the Sudan or its people out of my mind. I'd wanted so much to minister to the pastors, which is why when Ed Cornwell asked if I'd like to return, I quickly replied, "Yes!". Ed said he had begun to arrange a seminar for refugee Sudanese pastors across the border in Uganda—it would be safer there, he said.

But I didn't really care. I knew I was supposed to go.

❖ ❖ ❖ ❖ ❖

17

Nairobi:
A Near Miss & A Nightmare

*...in Your book they all were written,
the days fashioned for me, when as yet there were none.*

Psalm 139:16

In July of 1998 I prepared to fly to Nairobi, Kenya, and once again travel into the unstable territory of Uganda to lead a four-day Inductive Bible Study seminar for a large group of Sudanese pastors. On this trip, Debbie and Aaron (twelve at the time) decided to tag along with me. Since I thought it too dangerous for them to go into Uganda with me, they stayed at an American guesthouse in Nairobi, Kenya.

It took many hours of dry, hot, bumpy travel before our team finally made it to Uganda. Thankfully, the trip proceeded uneventfully, except for the enormous potholes.

Pastors came from near and far, some from incredibly brutal situations. Many had seen their homes torched and burned to the ground, while others' children had been raped, kidnapped, and sold into slavery. Most of them ended up leaving their homeland and moving across the border to refugee camps where they hoped to find a safe haven.

The ruthless and relentless rebels crossed the borders and attacked the refugee camps at will, until the Ugandan government finally stepped in and put a halt to it.

The Sudanese pastors showed up hungry to learn how to study the Bible. Although teaching them the process seemed extremely slow to me, they gradually began to understand the concepts of Inductive study.

After the seminar concluded, we headed back to Kenya. When we got to the border, we heard some news which made my stomach turn: the U.S. Embassy in Nairobi had been bombed, resulting in many deaths. I'd left Debbie and Aaron behind because it seemed safer!

I'd visited the bombed embassy and knew it sat in the middle of a popular downtown shopping area. I also knew Debbie wanted to do some shopping. Dreadful thoughts attacked me of Debbie and Aaron hurt in the blast—maybe even killed. During the next four hours of travel, I prayed. "Let them be all right, Lord. Please." I prayed they weren't near the bombing.

Fears filled my mind like poison gas. I never doubted God was in control. I also know, God is God and He does whatever He needs to do in His economy to glorify His name and fulfill His will. In fact, Debbie and Aaron could be dead.

As we pulled up to the American guesthouse compound in Nairobi, my heart pounded. Debbie and Aaron didn't keep me waiting long, as they came hurrying out to greet us.

I discovered they'd been near the embassy one day before the bombing. The day of the attack, they ventured to another part of town, but heard the explosion and knew we would worry about their welfare. After a prolonged family hug, our phone rang.

The joy of our reunion didn't last long.

The native pastor of Calvary Chapel Nairobi called to let us know his wife didn't come home after the bombing; they thought she'd been downtown near the embassy at the time of the explosion. Debbie met this couple at the guest house a couple of days before the bombing and enjoyed their company.

Our team immediately canvassed hospitals in the area. It took us two days to cover them all, but we could not find her. We reluctantly began searching the morgues.

After another two days of hunting we found her lifeless body lying in a large pile of corpses. The discovery devastated the pastor and his four children. The following Sunday we held a memorial service for her at the morning services — a sad and somber event for their entire church family.

A Safari Sabbath

Between the stressful trip to Uganda and death of the pastor's wife, our family needed a change of scenery, so we took advantage of a friend's generosity and went on a safari in Kenya.

Our safari exposed us to a tremendous amount of wildlife. As we motored down a winding dirt road, we pulled off to see several enormous elephants, one of which blocked the road. Our guide just stopped the vehicle and waited patiently for the elephant to move. It did take awhile!

"Never try to drive around them," he warned. "Sometimes they charge when you do that."

We definitely didn't want that. I could see the headlines now:

MISSIONARY FOOTBALL COACH ESCAPES DEATH IN BANGLADESH AND PHILIPPINES, BUT FAILS TO ELUDE CHARGING ELEPHANT IN KENYA!

Back in Nairobi after the safari, we spent our last night in a plush hotel, nearly vacant in the aftermath of the bombing. Prices had plummeted so we decided to splurge.

The next morning, as we enjoyed breakfast, Aaron spotted a grand piano in the dining area and disappeared. We soon heard praise music echoing through the room, followed by an encouraging round of applause. Aaron relished the attention and came back, smiling, to finish his breakfast.

18

Football in The Ukraine

*See, I have set before you an open door,
and no one can shut it.*

Revelation 3:8

What would happen if I ever got to put my two passions together—
football and Inductive Bible Study—for one cause, Jesus Christ? The
opportunity to find out came in the summer of 2002 when an old friend
and football-lover, Bill Clingwald, called to ask if I would coach an
evangelistic football team heading for the Ukraine. Bill made similar
trips in the past.

Our team would include former high school and college players, as well
as former NFL pro Todd Kitchen. The teams we would face in the
Ukraine belonged to an Eastern Europe semi-pro league. We would play
three advertised games over ten days, draw big crowds, and share the
gospel with everyone we met along the way.

Oh, and I would get to lead our team through the Inductive Bible Study
seminar.

How could I refuse?

My team trainer from ACA and good friend, Ben Mulder, agreed to join
us. After much planning and prayer, we took off for Kiev. Once our team
gathered, I had three days to teach my offense and defense. We had some

fine athletes, but not nearly enough of them. Several players backed out at the last minute, leaving us with just a twelve-man roster.

In Kiev, however, we met a group of young Ukrainian men who'd played on a team which disbanded; they were more than eager to join us. Although I explained everything through an interpreter who knew nothing about football, we communicated our points and all of us got fired up about hitting the gridiron for the ultimate purpose of sharing our faith.

We planned to have several players give their testimonies at halftime or after the games, then give those in attendance an opportunity to surrender their lives to Christ. Unfortunately, the organizer of the first two games misunderstood our intent and did no advertising for either contest. In our eyes, no advertising meant no crowds.

We couldn't help but feel discouraged.

We were to play our first game on a Sunday afternoon. Sunday morning, I was scheduled to speak at the worship services of Calvary Chapel Kiev. Before I got up to speak, a group of guest musicians from Southern California led worship. I got to thinking: These guys are good. I wonder if they'd consider coming over to play before this afternoon's game.

I held onto the thought while speaking to the congregation, but I did explain why we'd come to Kiev and invited everyone to come out to the game later in the afternoon. After the service, I talked with Danny Vann, the leader of the band, and asked if his group would like to play before the game.

Danny and his band gladly accepted the invitation. They got their gear set up and began jamming forty minutes before kickoff. The entire church came out to the game and with the loud music, many people felt drawn to the stadium. Several of us had an opportunity to share Christ before the game and during the half, so God worked out all the details despite the lack of publicity.

We even managed a win on the field.

Our second game disheartened us. Only a handful of people turned out and everyone felt down about it. We'd come so far, it all felt like a waste. Depression hit me.

Since there was virtually no crowd, we asked the other team if we could talk with them at halftime. They agreed. We shared Christ for about twenty minutes with some fifty players and fifty spectators. Several hands went up when we asked if anyone wanted to accept Christ. We led those people in the sinner's prayer.

We lost that game to a Ukrainian team far superior to us. Several of our guys got hurt, including our quarterback, who pulled a groin muscle and suffered severe pain. After the game the UK team joined us in payer for the injured players. What an extraordinary experience.

This event reminded me again about being faithful in the little things. When we are, He puts us in charge of more!

During our off times I lead the team through Inductive Bible Study course. We enjoyed many enriching hours of fellowship. Although we felt down about the small crowds, we pressed on and headed to our last stop, where we would have five days to let our wounds heal and prepare for the final game.

When our bus arrived at the hotel, the owner of the opposing team hopped on, told us how thrilled he was we'd come, and said he had a lot of plans lined up for the next few days. Many of his coaches and players knew the Lord and he hoped we might practice with his young players and teach them as much as we knew about football and walking the Christian life.

We settled in for a good night's rest and the spirit of the team lifted by the next day. We practiced with our opponent each afternoon, teaching the fundamentals of the game, and ended each practice with two or three of our team members giving their testimonies. The other team listened intently, especially to the NFL experiences of Todd Kitchen.

At the beginning of our stay, a Russian coach told one of our players he believed Christianity was for the weak. "I don't need that kind of crutch," he'd said. "I can make it through life perfectly fine without Him."

Later in the week, one of our big tackles, Gary Campbell, shared his faith. Gary is one enormous guy and his compassion spills over when he describes his feelings about Jesus Christ. When the Russian coach saw how a powerful young man like Gary relied completely on Christ, he felt touched. Later the coach told Gary he realized Christianity was not just for the weak. The coach proceeded to admit his need for Christ and soon invited Him into his life.

Game day arrived. As our bus approached the stadium, we were dumfounded to see hundreds of people lining up to get in. By kickoff, 10,000 spectators filled the place.

How else could we feel but ecstatic?

In the locker room before the game, we prayed together as a team. Shortly after we finished, two players from the other team walked into our locker room, fully dressed in their game uniforms, wanting to pray to receive Christ. "We don't want to wait till after the game," they said. What a way to start a game!

Only five minutes later, our exuberance turned to alarm. Just before we took the field, we learned local government officials, which sponsored the game, insisted we not share Christ at halftime. Since they hosted the event, they controlled what happened at the event. Many government officials would attend, and they forbade any proselytizing.

We were disappointed. They told us to expect formal player introductions at the beginning of the game and they wanted Bill and I to greet the crowd. They also wanted our NFL star, Todd Kitchen, to say a few words.

Bill and I did our thing, as directed, and thanked the large crowd for coming. Todd had something else in mind. He wasted no time, telling the intrigued crowd about his days making millions of dollars in the NFL, yet finding zero satisfaction from the money or the notoriety.

As Todd spoke for another ten minutes, sharing only through Christ he'd found peace and contentment. I scanned the crowd anxiously sure the hidden government officials would rise to shut us down. Todd ended his segment by telling the fans who wanted Christ in their lives to come down to see him on the field after the game.

And that was it. He'd gotten the gospel in and I knew it would not return void.

The game went on as scheduled and our quarterback, who could barely walk two days before, played the entire game. He thrilled the crowd with a fantastic air assault, including two long touchdown passes.

When the final seconds ticked off the clock, we'd won the game. People quickly crowded around Todd as he shared his faith, many came to Christ. It was a memorable day in the Ukraine!

❖ ❖ ❖ ❖ ❖

19

Bumps, Bruises, and Miracles in India

*If you have faith the size of a mustard seed,
you will say to this mountain
move from here to there, and it will move,
and nothing will be impossible to you.*

Matthew 17: 20

When I started planning a return trip to India in 2002, two pastor friends, Bill Barry and Paul Berry, expressed an interest in going with me. I was excited about the possibility. Both men were gifted teachers and I knew they would encourage the pastors. Paul had undergone open-heart surgery just nine months earlier and I wondered how he would hold up. Despite my warnings about the grueling trip ahead, he was determined to join us.

The three of us enjoyed traveling together. It took us three days to reach, Calvary Chapel of Eluru for our first pastors' seminar. We arrived late in the evening, enjoyed a good meal, and hit the sack. After a short time of rest, I woke up feeling sick to my stomach and spent the rest of the night in the bathroom.

All night I prayed for the Lord to intervene and heal me. The next morning, I still felt out of it, but several hundred pastors showed up for our first meeting and I didn't have the heart to cancel.

Somehow, God did give me the strength and endurance to teach the entire day. I dropped into bed that night, totally exhausted, and slept soundly.

We continued the seminar the next day; in the evening, Bill and Paul got invited to speak at a church way out in the country. The drive to the church took two hours and service lasted long into the night. They left the church in pitch darkness and inched their way to the car. As Paul walked around the vehicle, he fell into a deep ditch and badly hurt his leg. Bill enlisted some others to help Paul out of the ditch and into the car for a long bumpy ride back to our quarters in Eluru.

When they arrived early in the morning, they woke me to look at Paul's leg, because they knew I'd had experience with football injuries. But I couldn't gauge the severity of his injury; I saw no visible signs of trauma expect for some swelling. Still, Paul's leg hurt severely in two places. Fortunately, he'd brought pain relievers left over from his heart surgery. We got him started on those and tried to find a doctor but could find none. The only hospital nearby had limited medical resources... We couldn't even get our hands on any ice.

We prayed, and Paul spent the next day in bed with his foot elevated. We continued the seminar, and everyone pray for him. The next day Paul said his leg felt a little better, so we suggested he gently put some weight on it. There were no crutches or bandages available, but we wrapped it in an old Indian turban. He made it over to the church and even spoke the last day of the conference, a great encouragement for everyone.

From there, we traveled thirteen hours by car to our next seminar site where, all 500 seats in the conference room were filled. By late afternoon, 500 more pastors sat on the ground outside the building wanting to be a part of the seminar. Somehow, a group of illiterate ladies also found their way into the meeting room. They talked loudly during the sessions which became quite a distraction. When we politely asked them to sit outside, they became quite vocal and created a commotion as they left.

Hundreds of Hindus came from throughout the region to hear music and the gospel preached during our week-long evening crusades. Despite his hobbling, Paul participated and never once complained about his injury.

Ten days later when we returned to the States and Paul's leg was X-rayed. He learned he'd broken both the tibia and the fibula bones. The doctor said although he never would have recommended walking on the leg right after injury, as Paul did for two weeks, the pressure Paul put on the leg actually reset both of the bones, making surgery unnecessary! It would heal just fine.

God worked a wonderful miracle.

If we'd known the extent of Paul's injury, we probably would have cancelled the remaining seminar and crusade heading straight back to America. But, instead, God planned for us to minister to hundreds of pastors—and preach the Good News to many lost Hindus.

Amazing grace, how can it be?

Death to Life

Why don't we see more miracles in America? I have seen many wonders in Third World countries, such as India. I fear in the States, miracles are not only hard to come by, but they seem difficult for us to believe. Why is that?

Could it be unbelief within the church?

Or perhaps it's because we have so much in our country, we have lost the need to see God move in miraculous ways. We have our diverse medical plans, capable doctors, good hospitals, lots of "miracle" drugs, abundant food, and plenty of credit cards. The temptation, I fear, is to put our trust in those things rather than in God.

On the second day of our seminar in India, we conducted at a Bible school in Hyderabad for Gospel for Asia, I met a young pastor with an amazing story about our miracle working God. During lunch after much prodding, he reluctantly told me how he'd come to believe in Jesus Christ.

The young man came from the tiny country of Bhutan, packed with three million people, mostly Buddhists. The king of Bhutan would not tolerate the worship of any other gods. In his country, it was illegal to participate in any other religion except Buddhism.

As a youth, the young man's parents became believers by listening to Christian radio broadcasts. They freely and often told him about Christ, but he had zero interest. He cared nothing about their God (or Buddha, for that matter).

He grew up, got married, and soon to two boys enriched their lives. His young family lived together with his parents, a common practice in Bhutan. One day while on a business trip, he received a frantic call from his mother, saying his youngest son, an infant, had fallen deathly ill. They did not think he would live.

The young daddy rushed home as quickly as possible, but by the time he arrived, his baby boy died. The doctor, verifying his death, already left. The distraught father touched the cold, lifeless body of his flesh and blood, and wept. His son had died four hours earlier.

"Son," his mother squeezed his arm. "We've been reading in the Bible Jesus can resurrect the dead. We are going to pray over him right now —"

"Mom!" he cried. "If your Jesus will resurrect my son, I'll give my life to serve Him."

She and her husband laid hands on the baby. They prayed to God. Time passed. They continued.

And suddenly they felt a pulse.

They saw breathing.

And heard crying!

The baby returned to life. They called the doctor and he almost went into shock. When he pronounced the baby perfectly normal, this young father fell to his knees and gave his life to Jesus.

Today, he has started a number of underground churches and regularly records a series of Christian radio programs broadcast throughout the land. This young man fully realizes the government wants him dead.

"But I don't care," he insists, "God gave my son new life, and he gave me new life through Jesus. I must share."

What a profound impact his story has had on my life!

Opening Deaf Ears

Several years ago, when I conducted a seminar in Bangalore, India, one pastor kept coming up to me and sharing how much he enjoyed the conference. With great exuberance he expressed how freeing it felt to study God's Word and to be able to read and write.

Read and write? I thought. This guy is just so happy.

And then I heard his story.

I learned this man was born deaf and mute. Other children made fun of him constantly, called him names, pushed him, and threw rocks at him. By age nineteen he'd lost all hope and wanted to die. One Sunday he found a sturdy rope and marched out to a desolate area to hang himself.

Once he found the right place, far from other people, he set his sights on the first tree which looked strong enough to hold him. Just as he was about to hoist the rope over a large branch, something knocked him flat to the ground. He turned around to see who hit him but saw no one.

The same thing happened three times. Lifting himself from the dirt after his third unsuccessful try, he ran toward home, badly frightened. He came upon a church, stopped, and peered inside. He saw people singing, all of them happy and carefree. He could not understand it. Someone approached him and motioned him inside, as if to say, "Join us!"

He'd never visited a church before but entered and watched with great interest. Time passed and a group of worshipers gathered around him. They reached out, their eyes closed, and laid hands on him. They appeared to be praying to God. Praying. Praying — Pop.

He could hear — for the first time in his life!

The words came as clear as crystal: "Hallelujah, Hallelujah!"
Soon, his mouth repeated those words.

God healed him!

It took many years of diligent work for this young man to learn to speak, and afterwards to read and write. But he did it. Years later, God called him to become a pastor. And here he was, reading and studying God's Word in one of our Inductive Bible Studies.

As he told me his story, the words he repeated all week took on a whole new meaning: "Isn't it great to read and write and study God's Word?" Isn't it great, indeed!

❖ ❖ ❖ ❖ ❖

20

On to China

For whatever is born of God overcomes the world.
And this is the victory that has overcome the world — our faith.

1 John 5: 4

For more than a decade God put China on my heart. I wanted to get our Inductive Bible Study materials into the underground churches. For a time, it looked like there would be an opening, but the door closed when authorities arrested and imprisoned my contacts.

In the winter of 2003, someone contacted me about another possible "in" with the underground Chinese church. Arrangements looked very good for a training seminar and within a few months I was headed for the land of emperors and dragons!

I only had a small and brief window of opportunity, so I drew up plans. Because of the danger involved, I needed to keep quiet about the trip. I could not email my prayer team as I normally do before my travels and I could tell only a few close friends, supporters, and churches — so they could pray.

My contact told me the Chinese government has many spies in America and they often infiltrate churches. The government pays Chinese students attending school in America to visit U.S. churches, listen, and report any outreaches into China. They receive pay for their services.

I arrived in China, January 2004. I phoned our Chinese contact, who instructed me to go to a specific hotel. Once checked in, a couple in the hotel lobby motioned me over and told me to get ready for "pick up" the next evening.

A taxi picked me up the next night and drove some forty-five minutes to a group of apartment complexes. "Put your hood up and follow the man carrying a suitcase," I was told, "but do it at a distance." Feeling like Agent 007, I followed him a block or two, then up what seemed like five flights of stairs to a small apartment.

Once inside, several pastors who had arrived for the Inductive Bible Study warmly greeted me. They showed me my quarters, a small bedroom with no bed but several warm blankets. More pastors soon arrived.

For the next three days, no one left the apartment. We began our study each morning at 9 A.M. and continued until 9 P.M. We broke only for quick, simple meals, and then returned quickly to our studies.

The thirty pastors packed into the tiny apartment soaked up everything God revealed, like sponges. The IBS manuals was translated into Mandarin, so they didn't have trouble following along.

Many pastors in the underground Chinese church have little training and because of their limited understanding of the Bible, heresy has plagued the church. Some of the larger underground churches have made Bible school mandatory for new pastors, but often the people in leadership have limited knowledge. These men videotaped our entire seminar and planned to make hundreds of copies for their leadership.

It amazed me, a tremendous number of Chinese young people still want to become pastors, even though they know the danger of such a calling. They know they could end up in prison or labor camps, but it doesn't deter them.

Some pastors who get thrown into prison never come out. They are tortured frequently and have their sentences extended again and again. If they happen to have money, they can occasionally buy their way out; but most don't.

Many of the up-and-coming pastors in China are women. One reason is the wives of murdered and imprisoned pastors have picked up the torch and carried on.

I spent three days and nights in the cramped apartment, with thirty people sleeping shoulder-to-shoulder, no showers and just one bathroom. Although my body wanted to rebel, I could not complain. How could I, when I saw the staggering commitment of those pastors? They suffered dearly for the sake of the gospel. Once again, I realized how spoiled I am in America and how good we have it here. I wonder how many American Christians would be willing to become pastors if our country faced the same trying circumstances as do the Chinese.

The night we finished, my escort and I covered our heads and slipped into the night. A waiting taxi whisked us away. Two miles from the apartments, we switched taxis just to be safe, and the second one took us to my hotel. The steaming shower and soft bed felt almost too good to be true.

Two young men met me in the hotel lobby the next morning and we walked to a business center owned by Christians. One of the offices belonged to a large underground church.

For the next four days I conducted a second seminar for twenty more underground church leaders. Once again, we had a marvelous time digging into God's Word. It often amazes me how God rejuvenates my spirit and body each time I lead an IBS. I think it's because of the hungry souls He brings to the seminars from every walk of life.

They also videotaped the conference and sent it out to sister churches all over China. What a privilege! Virtually all of the underground churches in China are linked, so they share materials throughout the country. I found it hard to contain my excitement as we concluded two extremely powerful and meaningful seminars.

I took a day to tour the Great Wall of China, I couldn't help but ponder the fact this massive wall went up long before Christ, to keep out the enemy. The current government has tried relentlessly to keep Christianity out of China, but no wall or movement can thwart His love for mankind.

Upping the Ante

One year later I headed back to China, but through a different contact. One of the key leaders I'd worked with before had been arrested and imprisoned.

The Chinese government discovered a large warehouse owned by that Christian leader, filled with 300,000 Bibles and tons of Christian literature, including IBS materials and many videotapes of an entire IBS seminar. They confiscated all of it and because of the videotape, I probably became a target.

After making it safely through customs, my contacts met me and whispered I should follow them out of the airport on foot. I did so. I walked out into a damp, wet cold. We got through the parking lot and out to a main street where a van raced up alongside us, picked me up, and zoomed off.

We drove for two hours. The van dropped me at a home where the driver instructed me to hurry inside. I spent the next three days inside the home, never leaving. Thirty pastors and I worked together from early morning till late at night. I can't express in words how eagerly they learned.

When we stopped for meals, the participants found it amusing to watch me struggle with chopsticks. Often, someone would bring me a spoon, but I felt determined to learn and became somewhat proficient as the days passed.

The first night, they took me to a small bedroom, all my own. Wow, I thought, now we're talking. But a few seconds later I felt frigid air pouring in and realized my window was broken. The two-story home had no heat, so I often spent my breaks wrapped under the covers in my bed. The rest of the participants slept on the floor, men in one room, women in another. The meeting place offered one bathroom to share among all of us, and it did not have a Western-style toilet, just a hole in the floor. It made going to the bathroom quite a challenge.

All of the participants arose and began praying by 5 A.M. each day. They prayed for two hours, often weeping. On the last day of the seminar, as our time together wound down, everyone began weeping. I asked the translator why. "They are weeping because they are so grateful the Lord has brought them someone who could teach them how to study the Scriptures better," he said.

After we concluded, my host asked if I would like to spend the rest of the day and night at a hotel, where I could get a hot shower and rest before we began another seminar with a new group of pastors. I gladly accepted. It felt wonderful to stay in a heated room with a shower, a comfortable bed — and yes, even a Western-style toilet!

Best of all, perhaps, I went for a walk in the evening and found a McDonald's. After eating only rice and vegetables, rice and meat, and rice and eggs for ten days, a Big Mac, fries, and Coke tasted fantastic.

I slept soundly and awoke refreshed ready to start a new three-day seminar with another group of leaders.

After completing the second seminar, believers took me to a home where some thirty young people gathered in a large upstairs room, all of them Bible school students with young and innocent faces. Each of them knew their calling might well lead to persecution and even death. I spent the rest of the day helping them understand how to study the Scriptures.

The following day another vehicle transported me to an isolated area where about 100 pastors gathered for a retreat. When we arrived, we found the director of the event already preaching; he went on for about two hours. During a break I met the leader. He greeted me warmly but said through the translator they usually didn't like to invite Americans to speak, because they could go for only forty-five minutes.

"Can you speak for two hours?" he asked.

I assured him filling the time frame wouldn't be problem so for the next two hours I taught from the Gospel of Mark. We took a short break and they insisted I teach for another two hours. I explained, unfortunately, I needed to get to the airport to catch my flight back to America.

I have never forgotten their hunger for the truth of the Scriptures.

Update

Today, over 10 million Chinese Christians continue to be persecuted as are Christians in Pakistan, Sudan, Iran, Syria, Nigeria and other countries. China's passage of new religious laws by the government and the Communist Party have escalated the danger to churches and their pastors. House churches are accused of being in a cult and leaders are sent to labor camps, mental hospitals, and prison. Their churches are essentially demolished and destroyed. Despite all the persecution the church in China is flourishing and growing at an unprecedented rate. We need to continue surrounding our brothers and sisters in prayer.

21
Devastation

He will swallow up death forever,
and the LORD God will wipe away tears from all faces.

Isaiah 25:8

By March of 2006, Debbie and I were almost empty nesters. Three of our four children were grown and married, leaving Aaron as the last one at home. Although he graduated from high school in 1994, Aaron couldn't find real direction in life.

His learning disabilities kept him from pursuing a college education, so he jumped from job to job, trying to figure out where he fit in. Because of his great experience in high school, he often returned to Arrowhead Christian Academy to help out however he could. The students and faculty loved him and one of his favorite PE teachers often asked him to help with her class.

Our neighbor Don Bulak, got Aaron a job with the Forest Service, cleaning up trails and cutting down dead trees. Aaron didn't work with a group of model citizens. In fact, several of the men were ex-cons. One day, Aaron came home and told Debbie and I the guys just taught him how to hot-wire a car. We weren't thrilled.

If Aaron loved one thing during his years in the States, it was motorcycles. In the Philippines we had a small scooter; it didn't go fast, but Aaron loved sitting in front of whoever drove it.
All through high school Aaron desperately wanted to buy a motorcycle,

I refused. I told him he needed to stay healthy for football; and besides, motorcycles were dangerous. Drivers can't see them.

After graduating from high school, Aaron purchased his first bike, a Suzuki 250. I urged him to use extra caution. He recognized the dangers, but he loved to ride. One day he took a spill and scraped his arm badly, but no broken bones. Not long afterwards, to our relief, he sold the bike and bought a used car.

The car was no motorcycle. Ask any motorcycle fan and he'll tell you there's nothing like the feeling of riding a bike on the open road. Six months after he bought the car, Aaron traded it in for a powerful Kawasaki 650. Again, we urged him to use caution, to drive defensively. He promised he would and expressed how good riding the motorcycle made him feel about himself.

On the morning of March 22nd, 2006, Aaron told us he was going to the Department of Motor Vehicles (DMV) to renew his license, because it was set to expire the following day (his birthday). As he left, he stopped by to say goodbye to his mother, then found me in the front yard. After confirming when the DMV opened, he said goodbye and took off.

Aaron normally took back roads because he liked riding them more than the busier ones, but construction closed his normal route, so he drove the main highway.

Just two blocks from the DMV office, a car didn't see him and darted in front of his bike. He was going 45 mph and there was no chance to stop or even swerve. He hit the car and died shortly after impact.

A police officer came to our home three hours later. He found me working outside and asked if we could talk. I invited him in and as we sat in the living room, he told me what happened to our precious boy. When I broke the news to Debbie, we just held each other and wept.

It was so difficult to fathom this beautiful, dark-skinned young man of ours would never come home to us again.

For the past twenty-one years he'd been such an important part of our lives. He required a great deal of work and we had to constantly follow up on him, but we loved him dearly. His brother and sisters were all devastated.

The local newspapers carried the tragedy on the front page and our phone rang off the hook. Emails flooded in from Russia, Africa, the Philippines, New Zealand, and around the world. Word of the accident traveled so fast; it boggled our minds. For the past twenty years, after every seminar, I told the story of how we found Aaron and how we considered him a gift from God. His life had touched many.

And now wonderful friends and family touched us with compassion as we mourned.

More than a thousand people attended Aaron's memorial service—a powerful, heart-wrenching event which brought honor to Aaron as well as God. At the end of the service our pastor, Ed Rea, asked if anyone wished to rededicate their lives to the Lord or make a commitment to Christ for the first time. Hands raised all over the chapel from coworkers to football rivals.

A week later, Arrowhead Christian Academy held an all-school assembly to honor Aaron. One of his favorite coaches, Willie Guida, spoke of the importance of having a game plan for death.

"All of us are making plans for the future," Willie said. "Planning where we will go to school or work, what trips we will make, and what we will do over the weekend. But often our plans for death and the after-life are overlooked. Aaron made a plan for death; he knew where he was going."

Once again, many hands went up to receive Christ.

In the days and years following Aaron's death, our family continues to grieve. we have learned a great deal about the process. Each person grieves differently. Both of my parents have died, and Debbie has lost both of hers, a stepmother, and older brother. We agreed those painful losses are very different from experiencing the grief of our son's death. No parent expects to bury his or her own child.

Life goes on. But there will always remain an enormous hole in our hearts until the moment we see our Aaron again in heaven.

Tender Mercies: Debbie

The Psalmist says, "Oh Lord you have searched me and known me… .and are intimately acquainted with all my way…" Psalm 139:1-6

What a wonderful truth about God's character. Time and time again He's made this truth a reality in various seasons of my life. Aaron's death was one such occasion. On the day he was killed by a motorist an awful image flashed in my mind. I pictured him lying in the road slowly dying, alone. As his mother, my heart ached because I couldn't hold and comfort him in those final moments as he passed. This scene played over and over in my mind. I hid this toxic pain behind a locked door in my heart telling no one, not even Dan.

Five years later, I stopped by a small local fruit market first thing in the morning and as I was checking out a lady got in line behind me. She introduced herself as a friend of our eldest daughter Lela, expressed her condolences for the loss of our son, and asked if she could tell me a story regarding his death. I'd never met this lady before, but there was no one else in the check-out line and the cashier didn't seem to mind so I replied, yes.

This is what she told me: A friend of hers, who is a nurse at a local hospital, had just gotten off her night shift and was on her way home when she saw our son's accident. She jumped out of her car, ran to him and as he lay dying in the road, held him close. She was a believer. I was so overwhelmed by her tender story, I'm not sure if I thanked her or paid my grocery bill. A few minutes later I found myself sitting in my car sobbing with a grateful heart. God sent one of His messengers to communicate a story in a fruit market about His tender encompassing love at our son's death. He used a compassionate nurse to physically cradle him as he left this planet. I didn't need to be there, God had it covered! The hidden pain shut up in that dark closet of my soul was released and gone. What a gracious God who was intimately acquainted with a festering pain and chose to orchestrate circumstances for healing.

Running to Win

As I look back on my life and line it up with the Scriptures, I realize, God never promised us an easy life. He has promised to remain with us and never forsake us. The Bible brims with wonderful promises to help us through our toughest days. When the rough times come—and they will—God gives us a choice of becoming bitter and resentful, or acknowledging He is in control. His righteous promises giving us a future and hope are true!

Debbie and I are closing in on our fifth decade of marriage. One might assume for it to have lasted so long we have extraordinary compatibility. On the contrary. we've worked very hard communicating and living out what the bible commands: unconditional love. Our marriage has not been easy sailing. Serving as a football coach, pastor, and traveling missionary has put many challenges and pressures on our relationship and family.

God brought Debbie into my life to be my helpmate. That's just a fact. He looked down from heaven and said, "Dan, you are definitely going to need a lot of help—from someone very special and very patient!" It's taken me awhile, but I'm finally realizing He brought Debbie into my life as a teammate. Teammates have to work together to succeed and win. Each is valuable and essential in accomplishing God's game plan.

All of us are running a race.

You are.

I am.

Someday, I will cross the finish line.

And so, will you.

I long to hear those words I've read so often, words from the Master Himself: "Well done, thou good and faithful servant."

I believe Aaron will be one of the first to greet me. Knowing him, he'll probably run up and jump into my arms, yelling, "I beat you here!" He loved to win too.

I hope as you reflect on the stories in this book you will be encouraged to run the race to win.

"For we walk by faith and not by sight" (2 Corinthians 5:7).

That takes Intensive Faith!

❖ ❖ ❖ ❖ ❖

Epilogue
The Ministry Continues

Intensive Care Ministries began in the Philippines in 1985. I didn't understand at the time why God gave me the name. But since then, as I have seen firsthand the condition of the Christian church around the world and how God's Word is being diluted, I realize it's because the church needs "intensive care." It will become polluted and ineffective without the understanding of God and the truth of His Word.

"For the time will come when they will not endure sound doctrine, but according to their own desires, because they have itching ears, they will heap up for themselves teachers; and they will turn their ears away from the truth and be turned aside to fables" (2 Timothy 4: 3, 4).

I believe ICM is one of a number of ministries the Lord has raised up to challenge the church to teach God's Word in context, systematically. The majority of pastors around the world teach topically often taking one or two verses and jumping all over the bible to make a specific point they want to emphasize. An occasional topical message or series can be helpful but if that method is the only teaching format, the entirety of His Word is only partially communicated. Pastors have to search each week for a new subject to teach their congregations. But if they would simply work through the Bible, verse-by-verse and chapter-by-chapter, they would cover every topic!

Why does this seem like such a foreign concept in churches today?

Could it be, pastors are giving itching ears what they want to hear instead of obeying the words of Jesus when he said, "Sanctify them in the truth; Thy word is truth" (John 17: 17).

Intensive Care Ministries

Intensive Care Ministries works in many countries around the world. The IBS course has been taught in 54 countries. We currently have directors in Africa, India, Pakistan, Philippines and South America. The Inductive Bible Study materials have been translated into more than fifty languages. Numerous American pastors from a variety of churches have taught the IBS materials in countries such as Cuba, Indonesia, Thailand, Tonga, New Zealand, Tahiti, and Romania. We now have five Bible schools in Africa where national Sr. Pastors go through a rigorous three-year IBS course. The classes are mostly taught by qualified African pastors.

This ministry continues to be supported by churches, businesses, and individuals. Various doors of opportunity have opened to teach the IBS seminar in U.S. churches and Bible schools. Visit our website to learn more: www.icmbible.com

Our family

Many people have inquired about our three surviving children. They have all grown up and given us ten wonderful grandchildren and two new great grandchildren.

Our oldest daughter, Lela, is married to Frank Sanchez, the Senior Pastor of Calvary Christian Fellowship in Colton, California. Lela keeps busy supporting her husband in church ministry, teaching in public school and overseeing three daughters and a son. Renae, Caleb, Elizabeth and Anna. She is involved in worship and ministry with women.

Our second daughter, Corrie, is married to Chris Marquardt. Corrie is a full-time teacher and Chris is a pipe inspector. They are the parents of four, two girls who are grown and married, Hope and Hannah, and two boys still in school, Adam, and Isaiah both attending my old stomping grounds, ACA in Redlands, California.

They are involved at Wildwood Calvary Chapel in Yucaipa, California.

Our son, Nathan, worked has a worship pastor and creative arts director in several churches over the years. He now has his own business, Finfrock Web Design. His wife, Alyssa, assists in the business and home schools their two active children, Malachi and Kara. They live in Tehachapi, California and attend church there.

❖ ❖ ❖ ❖

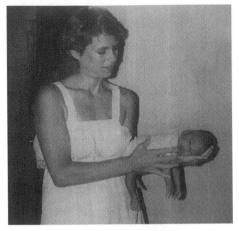

April 1985
Aaron at one month old

November 2003
Dan & Aaron ACA Football

April 1990
Kindergarten

June 2004
Aaron High School Graduation

Debbie and Dan married for 49 years.

Sanchez Family (L-R)
Renae, Anna, our daughter Lela, Frank,
Caleb and Lizzie

Marquard Family (L-R)
Chris, our daughter Corrie, Adam & Isaiah

Finfrock Family (L-R)
Alyssa, Kara, Malachi and our son Nathan

Bonneville Family (L-R)
Granddaughter Hope, great granddaughter Nova and Marc

Mann Family (L-R)
Granddaughter Hannah, great granddaughter Maddox and Josh

What a joy to witness the next generation growing up

and training their children to love God,

as He commanded the children of Israel long ago: "....

love the Lord your God with all your heart,

and with all your soul, and with all your might."

Deuteronomy 6:5